Radio Programming in Action

Radio Programming in Action

Realities and Opportunities

Edited by Sherril W. Taylor
Vice President for Radio, National Association of Broadcasters

COMMUNICATION ARTS BOOKS

HASTINGS HOUSE, Publishers • New York 10022

Copyright © 1967, by Hastings House, Publishers, Inc.

All rights reserved. No part of this book
may be reproduced without
written permission of the publisher.

Published simultaneously in Canada
by Saunders, of Toronto, Ltd. Don Mills, Ontario

Library of Congress Catalog Card Number: 67–21431

Printed in the United States of America

CONTENTS

Preface 9

PART ONE:
NEWS AND PUBLIC SERVICE
    Modern Radio's Major Role—Large Markets   13
1. Merrill M. Ash
    Radio News Director, KIRO, Seattle, Washington   15
2. Dominic R. Quinn
    Program Director, WEEI Radio, Boston, Massachusetts   23
3. Paul B. Marion
    Vice President and Managing Director, WBT Radio, Charlotte, North Carolina   27
4. Vern Mueller
    Program Director, KPOJ Radio, Portland, Oregon   36
5. Jim Bormann, News Director, WCCO Radio, Minneapolis, Minn.   42

PART TWO:
NEWS AND PUBLIC SERVICE
    Modern Radio's Major Role—Small Markets   47
  6. Richard Jackson
    President, WBEC, Pittsfield, Massachusetts   49
  7. John H. Lemme
    General Manager, Radio KLTF, Little Falls, Minnesota   56
  8. Julian Haas
    President, KAGH, Crossett, Arkansas   62
  9. John H. Hurlbut
    President, WVMC, Mt. Carmel, Illinois   67
  10. George J. Volger
    General Manager, KWPC, Muscatine, Iowa   74

PART THREE:
MODERN MUSIC   81
  11. John R. Barrett
    Station Manager, KRLA, Pasadena, California   83
  12. Perry B. Bascom
    General Manager, WBZ Radio, Boston, Massachusetts   89
  13. Danny Williams
    Program Manager, WKY, Oklahoma City, Oklahoma   93

PART FOUR:
COUNTRY MUSIC   99
  14. Dan McKinnon
    President, KSON, San Diego, California   101
  15. George G. Dubinetz
    Vice President and General Manager, WJJD, Chicago, Illinois   104
  16. R. E. "Bob" Thomlinson
    General Manager, KTAR, Eugene, Oregon   112
  17. Dale Peterson
    General Manager, KGBS Radio, Los Angeles, California   116
  18. Jerry Glaser
    Director, Country Music Association   120

Contents 7

PART FIVE:
"BEAUTIFUL" MUSIC 125

19. F. Geer Parkinson
    Vice President and Station Manager, WRYT,
    Pittsburgh, Pennsylvania 127
20. Wally Nelskog
    President and General Manager, KIXI, Seattle,
    Washington 131
21. Gil Bond
    General Sales Manager, KIXI, Seattle, Washington 133

PART SIX:
FM RADIO 137

22. Lynn A. Christian
    General Manager, WPIX-FM, New York, New York 139
23. Robert Bruton
    Program Director, WFAA Radio, Dallas, Texas 146
24. Everett B. Cobb
    General Manager, KNEV, Reno, Nevada 149

PART SEVEN:
THE SPORTS BONANZA 153

25. Bob Cheyne
    Sports Publicity Director, University of Arkansas 155
26. Bert S. West
    Vice President and General Manager, KVI, Seattle,
    Washington 162
27. Allan Newman
    Program Director, KSFO, San Francisco, California 171

Index 175

PREFACE

BROADCASTERS all over the United States are filled with confidence and enthusiasm about the future of radio. The next five to ten years promise to be a time of dynamic growth and development, surpassing the prophecies of even the most optimistic among us. In fact, radio has already crossed the threshold of this great growth period.

This optimism is due in no small part to new creativity in radio—new uses of the art and imagery of sound.

In the decade since its crucial, but as it turned out, artificial, encounter with television, radio has been building the foundations for a major transition . . . a change of character and personality that is only now becoming apparent. Broadcasters have probed into the metaphysics of radio, asking themselves, "What can radio do best?" It was this introspection that marked the beginning of what Arthur Hull Hayes of CBS Radio has called "the newest mass medium."

The music-and-news format, the uniquely personal disc jockey, and such latter-day innovations as talk and open-mike programs recaptured and then far outstripped the big audiences of radio's so-called heyday. The emergence of substantial, authoritative news operations brought to the medium a permanent, daily importance in the lives of Americans. Listening habits changed, too: listening became an individual rather than a family activity; tune-in peaks shifted to new hours; and, with the debut of the transistor, radio became pocket-sized and truly portable.

In short, radio began to offer a new, steadily more personal service to its audience, and they accepted it overwhelmingly.

Tomorrow's radio programming will continue to be directed towards large but specialized audiences. Stations will take on clearly defined personalities as they cater to the information needs and entertainment tastes of one or more specific social groups.

Another major trend closely allied to the refinements in programming is the enhancement of production values. Striking new concepts are emanating from what Dr. A. William Bluem of Syracuse University calls "the forgotten art" of communication by sound. In its pre-television days, radio enchanted audiences with word-and-sound pictures of characters, settings and ideas. Today we are witnessing a renaissance of this art-form. People like Tony Schwartz and Eric Siday are experimenting in the fields of electronic music.

The following papers, delivered on modern radio programming, point up the new exciting role of radio, emphasize the diversification of programming and program concepts in the medium.

The words are written by some of the most illustrious day-to-day practitioners of the new radio, the new art and imagery of sound. These broadcasters reside in widely scattered parts of the United States and represent different sizes of markets. They broadcast a variety of popular new formats, each designed to fill the particular needs of his community.

SHERRIL W. TAYLOR

Washington, D. C.
July 1967

Radio Programming in Action

PART ONE

News and Public Service

Modern Radio's Major Role

Large Markets

1. MERRILL M. ASH
   Radio News Director, KIRO, Seattle, Washington

2. DOMINIC R. QUINN
   Program Director, WEEI Radio, Boston, Massachusetts

3. PAUL MARION
   Vice President and Managing Director, WBT Radio, Charlotte, North Carolina

4. VERN MUELLER
   Program Director, KPOJ Radio, Portland, Oregon

5. JIM BORMANN
   News Director, WCCO, Minneapolis

In order to be granted in the first place and then keep a licence to operate, radio stations in the United States are required by the Federal Communications Commission to serve the needs of their communities by day-in, day-out, conscientious public service. Stations, which normally do the most outstanding job of public service and news programming, are also usually the most successful economically.

There's a good reason for this. Curiously, it seems to have developed in radio when television entered the scene almost 20 years ago. News and public service together are a commodity of programming which radio can do with unmatched facility.

Radio can get the story and present it while it's actually happening. *Voices, human interest, background sounds are all used spontaneously to communicate happenings which affect the lives of the citizenry.*

With the advent of television, when radio had to rebuild its personality and find new ways to survive and grow, news and public service took on new prominence.

This two-part section, grouped for convenience into large markets and small markets, includes detailed studies on news and public service from a number of top station practitioners from all over the United States. The comments are frank—even critical—and they all reflect the great desire to do a consistently better job of news and community service.

1

MERRILL M. ASH

At the time he wrote the following paper, Mr. Ash was News Editor of KIRO Radio, Seattle, Washington. He later joined the Boeing Aircraft Company. Prior to joining KIRO, Mr. Ash held similar positions at KOMO, Seattle and KOL, Seattle.

I HAVE BEEN called a hard-headed, uncompromising purist. I plead guilty. I believe that to compromise with news is to compromise with truth, ethics and integrity, and any compromise in these areas is the same as being a "little bit pregnant." It just isn't practical.

A Seattle newspaper columnist has referred to me as "one of the happy refugees from broadcasting."

I am leaving the industry after almost 30 years and about 20-thousand newscasts. I am *not* a "happy refugee from broadcasting." I am *not* a "happy refugee from" my present station. I am a reluctant but a determined refugee from the *industry*. Some of my reasons should be apparent a little further on.

My three decades in radio news have not been totally without reward. I have learned what radio news can be and sometimes is.

If there is one way radio can compete with the boob tube it is in the field of news.

Radio is fast. The tube is slow.

Radio is *news*. The tube is show.

Radio takes one man and a few thousand dollars. The tube takes many men and hundreds of thousands of dollars.

Radio gets to those who can listen and think. The tube sits and looks back at the mouth breathers.

A so-called reporter in Seattle was sent to the airport one day in 1957 to talk with attorney Robert Kennedy, who was to become the Attorney General. He was coming to Seattle to look into the affairs of the Teamster's Union under the famous Dave Beck. He poked his microphone into Kennedy's face and asked this deathless question: "Mr. Kennedy—are you an attorney?"

A few weeks later Mr. Beck returned from Washington where he had appeared before the Senate Crime Investigating Committee. Another so-called reporter shoved a microphone in his face and said: "Mr. Beck. I don't know what is going on—I haven't been paying any attention to the news, but what is the situation?"

Now here are some quotes I have collected from program directors I have known:

"Who, in his right mind, would ever listen to local news when he can listen to the network and hear reports direct from Cairo or London?" I heard that first about 15 years ago.

"I don't care who is on trial or how big you think the story is. The owner of that new market is a good sponsor and you are going to cover his grand opening. It's probably the big news story of the year."

"Of course you can't go to the National News Directors' Convention. Who cares that much about news, anyway?"

"So—call in the story from the next room and use wire copy. Nobody will know the difference and you won't have to leave the building."

If there is a program director who hasn't used one or more similar statements—more than once—congratulations. The whole theme, too often, is: "Nobody cares, anyway. Just shut up and let us play the music—or put on the telephone talk expert—or, rip it off the wire and read it. That's why we have AP."

If there is any one area which radio must support and strengthen in order to hold its own in the growing electronic competition, it is in the field of news. Rock and roll sells the kids. Carefully programmed music and informational programs can sell the adults. A reputation for ethical, carefully written, thoughtfully presented, balanced news can do more to hold a quality image than any other one ingredient.

With the advent of the easily portable tape recorder and the acquisition of "beeper" recording equipment by every radio station, there was a boom in coverage of local news stories by local radio staffs. However, because of the dearth of true reportorial talent, not only has the caliber of radio news coverage been dropping the past few years, but the quantity. I am sure part of the answer is the habit many radio managements have acquired of downgrading the talents necessary in a true *news*man. Too many station managers and program directors have the attitude that the only areas requiring talent are those of the dj and sales. They often feel that anyone, *by mere designation as such,* can be a newsman; anyone is capable of knowing a news story; anyone can interview anybody on any subject adequately enough for a local newscast.

I was told recently by the owner of an independent Seattle area radio station that "interviewing is simple." All you have to do is ask the interviewee's age, home town and hobbies—and that should wrap it up. This statement was made seriously by a man who was trying for a rather important news contract with a big company. His newsman (so called) is a full-time disc jockey with a tape recorder at hand for emergency coverage of the really big stories such as supermarket openings and new branch bank manager interviews. If you happen to represent the type who seriously cares about the age, home town and hobbies—and that is all—of presidents, ambassadors, senators, representatives, princes, scientists or what have you, you are this man's ideal audience. Even if this represented the entire range of your curiosity, surely you would like to hear the questions asked by someone who sounded as though he cared—and wasn't just killing time between records.

Even the program director or station manager who is a good showman and nothing else (and more power to him) should be able to see the value in a careful, probing interview of a personage who has something to say, if the newsman is smart enough to bring it out. In order to do so, however, he has to be a dedicated *news*man—not interested in presenting just a "show," but interested only in stimulating his interviewee to answering questions for the purpose of informing his listeners. Not entertaining. I said—*informing*. And seldom the twain shall meet.

This is where the dedicated newsman and the run-of-the-mill program director and station manager part forever. News is not, cannot, must not be contrived, distorted, changed to any degree from its inherent, factual, informational integrity for the sake of "showmanship." It must not, cannot ethically, be made funny when it is inherently tragic. It cannot be made "human interest," whatever that may be, if it is general interest. It cannot be made clean and light and happy if it is dirty, deep and bitter—if it is. If one tries—with gimmicks, gadgets and inflections—to make it what it is not, then one is a liar. That one is despicable and not deserving of the title of *news*man.

That is what is wrong with broadcast news today, and that is where the program directors and station managers who have the final say over broadcast news today often make a fatal and irrevocable mistake.

And it is a mistake. For even the wildest, rock and roller can build a reputation for news integrity. I know. I have done it. And, until the owner put all his bets on a wild-one from the heart of the Bible Belt, ratings were up, sales were up, income was high and the station standing—in spite of its music—was respectable. The "wild-one" from a Southern state—a sort of a program director, who did not deserve that honorable title—succeeded in bankrupting the station in eight short months.

Too often station managements justify a weakness in their news presentation with the statement: "We're a music and news station." If only they would say, proudly: "We're a music and *news* station."

What kind of people listen to news? What kind of people listen to music? Two different kinds of people? Do we have over on this side of the fence a great, faceless throng which listens only to music? And on this side do we have another throng which listens only to news? Hardly. I listen to music. You listen to music. Do you never listen to news? Do you never want to know what is happening in the world around you?

Do you *know* that a newscast is an unwelcome interruption of your program format? Do you know that you *must* have your dj's apologize for 30 seconds before the news with the comment: "Just hang around now. We'll be back right away—right after the news. Don't go 'way now. Just stand by. Little 'ole you-know-who will be right back with another one of those nifty little goodies hot off the turntable . . . and now the news." Do you *know* that the news itself will not be of sufficient interest to hold your listeners—that you must drag them somehow through the period with a singing introduction and a singing sign-off and beeps, whistles and shouts all the way through?

If you *know* this, if there is no doubt in your mind, then you darn well need a new news director, or he needs a new program director—or you both need a new boss.

News directors have conventions, professional societies, organizations devoted to raising standards and improving the over-all quality of news presentation. Do you know who goes to those conventions? Program directors charged with the task of finding a new gimmick, a new hook for presenting the news go to them. They return to home base filled with all the wrong ideas, and the news director quietly opens his veins on the boss's carpet. And the beeps and the whistles and the frantic urgency of the news grows a little worse, and its integrity a little less, and its image a little more grim. And that is radio news.

But that need not be radio news, and it is *not* news on *all* radio. So, where do we go from this low point? Up! How? Money, training, equipment, money, brains, work and—complete *hands-off* by the entertainment area of broadcasting.

First, money—money to hire newsmen-reporters. I do not mean "reporters" in the sense the word is often used in radio—to describe a man who "reports" on the air. I mean a "reporter" in the traditional sense of a man who knows news, who never sees an unusual occurrence without asking "why?" and "how?"

How do you find such talent? You pay for it. Who finds it? A competent, experienced, news director who may have had his training in radio but who, in spite of that fact, has developed a burning urge to be ethical, honest and to learn something about everything—and tell all to whomever will listen. You let him do the hiring and the instructing and the assigning of the men he tells you are reporters. If their voices aren't the best, if they have no sympathy for the troubles of your dj's but if they are willing to climb out of bed at 3:00 A.M. on a stormy morning to talk with a rescued sailor, or an injured fireman, or a survivor of a plane crash—and do so sympathetically and in a way which brings forth all the information—it may just be you have a news staff.

How much must you pay? That depends on your area. Certainly you must pay more for a competent *broadcast* newsman than is paid for hack reporters at the *Daily Blunder,* who have only to call in the barest skeleton of the story, have it written and rewritten, edited and re-edited by experts before it is in print. Your man has to go to the scene, interview expertly, write skillfully, voice fluently—all under pressure the newspaper reporter has never experienced. And, because he can be instantly identified by his interviewees and his listeners as the one man in between, he has to take the brunt of all the criticism which may be stimulated by any worthwhile story. Your newspaper reporter, in the main, is anonymous—so much so his editor may not be able to attribute the authorship of any specific story at any given moment. Try that on *your* news department.

As to training. That's difficult. Again, however, if you start with the right material your news director can do the shaping. Some stations insist on a degree in journalism. One station I know insists on a degree in political science—but no experience. I disagree. Far more important than degrees is the natural curiosity of the man himself, diluted to some degree by judgment, aided by skillful direction, lubricated by sympathy and empathy, and controlled by a certain amount of skepticism.

I also mentioned brains. I only wish I knew how and where to find that ingredient. I keep trying. Money isn't necessarily the answer here.

I mentioned work. I mean work—legwork, pounding the marble halls and cement corridors of your city's hospitals, police department, court house, city hall, climbing the stairs in your chamber of commerce, padding through the corridors of your main hotels, checking, checking, checking on a daily, hourly basis every city, county, state and federal official in and near your town. A good reporter knows them all on a first name basis, but he never lets his listeners know that he calls them anything but Mayor, Chief, Mr. Prosecutor, Judge or Sir. But, he *knows* them all and he knows the first names of their secretaries, their habits, "where the body is buried." And, he knows their bosses' names and habits, and he knows their enemies and why they are enemies. He uses every scrap of information he has for the one purpose—to cover the news.

To a good newsman there can be but one religion—it is the creed of accuracy and unswerving dedication to the ideal of complete news coverage of every newsworthy person and event in your city.

One thing will drive him away. Meddling in that creed in the name of "showmanship"—one of the nastiest words to a newsman that was ever coined. There is another thing which can drive him away. That is being pushed constantly to do more than he can possibly accomplish *properly*. And that, too, is a failing of radio news departments. The answer to that I have not found. It may be in the area of more money—for staff.

Some of you may want a few specifics: my idea of what a good, minimum metropolitan news department needs in the way of manpower and equipment.

First—manpower. A minimum of a news director—one with experience, ambition, consistency and imagination—and one man inside and two outside for each shift covered. The news director can be one of the two outside men during his shift, if necessary. Sometimes it is preferable.

Another requirement for a good news operation is a rule that never shall a newscast be prepared or read by anyone other than a newsman. The surest way to sound mediocre is to allow the dj to throw something together from the wire and read it as a "newscast." It isn't that. It isn't much of anything, really. If you must make your men double up, at least give the news reader—the "talking head"—a chance to look over his copy without distraction and give him some direction so he has a vague idea of what you want.

Equipment. This can vary greatly. The need for fancy equipment varies inversely with the ability and imagination of your news department. There are certain basic tools, however. A beeper tape recording device for recording from the telephone and a minimum of three portable tape recorders for the outside men—two going, one in reserve. The news department must have access without restriction to full dubbing facilities for editing tapes and preparing them for broadcast. The department also should be equipped with the necessary radios for receiving all your local emergency broadcasts—fire, police, sheriff, state patrol or what have you. No department should be without at least one mobile unit equipped with some sort of two-way communication with the newsroom and with a radio tuned to the local police frequency. Elementary—but often overlooked—is the need for a private telephone line direct to the newsroom with an unlisted number. Both news wires are also a necessity. Too many managements feel they duplicate each other. That is not true. They complement each other.

The newsmen you have are the important ingredient and you won't keep them without paying them. Seattle broadcasting has lost 150 years of irreplaceable experience to the higher salaries paid by industry in the past 12 months. Within the next six months I expect the industry to lose another 150 years of experienced personnel. These men won't be replaced by the kids from Colville, Grants Pass, Shamokin, Colfax or Pullman. This experience and dedication are gone forever and their disappearance from broadcasting, at a rate about 500% faster than normal attrition, is going to hurt. Not all managements realize this yet, but they will. And then they will wonder where the ratings went.

2

DOMINIC R. QUINN

Currently director of programming of WEEI, Boston, Massachusetts, Mr. Quinn is a graduate of Loyola University, Chicago, Illinois. He has served as program manager of KDKA, Pittsburgh, WIND, Chicago and WINS, New York. Also, he's worked as an announcer, newsman and disc jockey.

UNTIL ABOUT A year ago WEEI, a 5,000-watt CBS-owned station in Boston, could have been described as "three stations in search of a format." Having enjoyed for many years a commanding position in the Boston market, WEEI, by the end of 1963, was, for all practical purposes, a non-entity. It had a loyal, hard-core audience, but the trouble was that old listeners were all dying off with the result that, in the early days of 1964, there were times when I could have reached a larger audience simply by the opening of my office window and hollering across the Boston Common. WEEI was not one station but three: it was one station in the morning with a conventional program of music and news and chatter; it was another station in the afternoon, with a rather straight-laced telephone show; and it was still a third station at night and on weekends, when it played a rather bland diet of middle-of-the-road popular music. Three different stations in the same day on the same frequency, and none of them could buy an audience.

For two quite simple reasons: We were doing nothing that

was distinctively our own; and what we were doing, others were doing much better. We had to find something that we could do well, and something which no one else was doing.

We found it in news and information.

We do it all day, from six in the morning till 11:30 at night, Monday through Friday: from six in the morning till ten in the evening on Saturday, and from ten in the morning till six in the evening on Sundays. And so now we are *one* station, Boston's only news and information station. When listeners want music, as they often do, they have their choice of several music stations. But, when they want to find out what's going on, when they need information, when they need help, or when they want to speak their mind, they come to WEEI.

If we're going to be a news and information station, it follows that we should give news a prominent part in our broadcast day—and we do. From six to nine every morning, Monday through Saturday, we present Boston's only three-hour news and information program. We call it the AM Report. We also have the midday report, 15 minutes at noon, and the PM Report, an hour and a half, at 6:00 P.M. On the AM Report we use three men, two newsmen and an anchor man, and deliver 10-minute newscasts on the hour and the half hour, followed by three minutes of sports and three of weather.

One of the first big problems we had to solve was: "Now that we've done the news, sports and weather, what *else* are we going to do?" This, to my mind, is the central problem in any extended news period. How do you use the remaining 15 minutes of any half-hour segment? We do it with regular pre-recorded news features. The deputy director of the Apollo Project reports for us every day on new developments in science. The chief of Harvard's Department of Nutrition reports on food and health. We have a five-minute business news sponsored by General Electric, but the main job of writing and producing the meat and potatoes news features falls to our newsmen.

The most popular feature every morning is an example of something you don't often hear on radio these days: a piece of *interpretive reporting*. It's done by Paul Benzaquin, newspaperman, author, and WEEI's leading talkmaster.

Paul Benzaquin's show, from two till six every weekday afternoon, is Boston's leading talk show. In a recent Greater Boston Pulse, he knocked off the two leading rockers in most segments. He runs, as do all WEEI talkmasters, on open-forum program, a hometown hall in which any responsible person can stand up—or call up—and speak his mind. This allows us to get a pretty clear picture of how most people feel about the events and issues of the day.

Now, a WEEI talkmaster can't content himself with being *only* a kind of electronic gadfly. You have to do more than just "put on" the whole town. Among other things, you have to realize that some news stories are just too good to leave to the newsmen. A talkmaster has to get on them while they're hot.

There's no better way to bring the old town-meeting into reality these days than by means of the open-forum telephone program on radio. Before the phone company developed a new set-up for us, we were limited to one irate listener at a time. Now when a listener reaches the boiling point, she calls WEEI and, like as not, we can put her in touch with another caller who thinks she's had an overdose of stupid pills.

We've found, too, that a WEEI talkmaster has to be more than a devil's advocate, more than a "let's you and him fight" type. He ought to be something more than a glib wise-guy trading insults with listeners whose only point in calling—or listening—is to hear how he's going to insult someone, or what will make him lose his temper today.

We've found it's better to try to help people when they ask for it. We found that a lot of listeners really need help. Mostly the help they needed was for good information. Whom to call? Where to go? What to say? What forms to fill out? What is the law? What are the rules? The average citizen in a society as complex as ours simply can't cope with big government. He needs a friend at court, someone he can turn to who knows the ropes at City Hall or on Beacon Hill. He's got one at WEEI. We try to put such a caller in touch with the public official who can answer his questions, give him the background information he needs. In this case, the man with the information was the State Registrar of Motor Vehicles who was listening to the program.

A WEEI talkmaster is a much harder man to replace on

vacation than is the average disc jockey. You can't just let anybody conduct an open forum. We decided last year to give a poor but honest cartoonist a chance to see what he could do. His name was Al Capp. Later, we invited another name well-known to Boston, Father Norman O'Connor, the "Jazz Priest." As a jazzman, Father O'Connor doesn't dig Lawrence Welk, and said as much several times.

So, the name of the game is News and Information . . . but, I never saw an FCC rule which said you're not allowed to have some fun with it whenever you can.

3

PAUL B. MARION

Mr. Marion attended public schools in Charlotte, North Carolina, graduated from Davidson College and did graduate work at Columbia University. He joined Jefferson Standard Broadcasting in 1952 as promotion manager of WBT and WBTV. He became general sales manager of WBT Radio in 1956 and in 1960 was named managing director of that station. He became a vice president of the Jefferson Standard Broadcasting Company in 1965.

WBT is a 50,000 watt full service station on 1110 kc and has been on the air over 44 years. Charlotte is located in the heart of the Piedmont Carolinas. The city of Charlotte has a population of 250,000 people, and the home county of Mecklenburg has approximately 320,000 people. Charlotte is 10 miles from the South Carolina line, and our WBT transmitter is approximately one and one-half miles from the state line. The area served by our half milivolt signal encompasses over two million people.

To me, the big challenge we have in presenting our news, and to a lesser degree all of our programming, is to maintain a balance between the primary metro area of Charlotte and the outside area of approximately 40 counties in North and South Carolina. The fact that we are on a state line presents additional problems and particularly in the area of news. Our job is a little more difficult than the metro stations in maintaining this balance between purely Charlotte news and area news. Fortunately, there is a great deal of interest in the outside area of certain types of local news. As Charlotte is the central city of this approximately 75 mile radius, there is interest from the outside area in news that pertains primarily to entertainment, financial, transportation, new and expanded facilities, health and education, sports events, and news that would have a direct bearing on the outside area. Conversely, there is almost no interest in news such as traffic conditions in the suburban area, city and county government stories that are purely in nature, minor accidents, fires, and news of this nature. Consequently, it takes a very thorough editing job to maintain a balance in our locally originated newscast and bulletins.

To compete successfully in the outside coverage area, we have to maintain at all times a large and reliable group of stringers throughout the entire coverage area. We cannot attempt to compete with each of the 100 stations in our basic service area on minor local news stories originating in each town and each county. Obviously, a major spot story such as a train wreck, bad accident or explosion would be a primary news story regardless of where it took place. All stations would eventually get this type story, but our problem is to get it first and factually from our stringer correspondents. The more difficult part of this "local area coverage" is where there is an internal story in a community in our coverage area of sufficient interest for us to do an in-depth reporting job. The type I am referring to here is acquisition or large expansion of an industry, for instance. These few explanations should give you a pretty good idea of what I am referring to as "balance" in all of our newscasts.

The second problem, somewhat peculiar to our station, is that we are serving two states with approximately 60% of our listeners in North Carolina and 40% of our listeners in South Carolina. Obviously, the majority of the news would hold equal interest to both states. However, the one area that this varies rather widely is in the assignment of "politics." As you know, the South generally has had some important changes in political alignments in the last few years and this is particularly true in South Carolina. This factor is so important to us that we assign different men to cover the political beats in each state. We also get wire service splits for both states. Obviously, having the two-state coverages means that we have to staff each legislature, each political convention, each major political race in both states as well as stay close to the political leaders that make news in the two states. This is handled by assigning a man on our own staff who knows this subject well. Also, we have a very strong stringer in each state capital. Naturally, when the legislature is in session, extra manpower is assigned to Raleigh and/or Columbia. The North Carolina legislature meets on a bi-annual basis, while South Carolina meets annually.

I think you will be interested in some of the "nuts and bolts" of our day-by-day news operation. Our news department is one of two combined departments serving both WBT Radio and WBTV Television. The other department consists of talent staff which works for both stations. We have 14 full time people in our news department, with 10 of these working for both radio and television. The four who do not work radio are primarily concerned with the photographic end of the TV news business.

Our news manager, Erv Melton, is in complete charge and reports directly to top management. Our news department is manned Monday through Saturday, from 6 A.M. until midnight. Throughout each of these six days per week, there is a radio editor on duty as well as a TV editor. Between midnight and 6 A.M. one newsman is assigned "on call" duty and police, fire, state highway and other radios are monitored. The same procedure is used on Sunday which, as you know, is primarily a day for spot news. A briefing is held at 8 A.M. each morning with the news manager and the news editor to discuss the upcoming day's news assignments. A second meeting is held at 2 P.M. each day to re-evaluate the day's news and the upcoming night assignments. While there is no deadline for radio news and our microphones are open on a moment's notice, our major effort goes in our 7 A.M., 12 noon, 6 P.M., and 11 P.M. newscasts. We are particularly conscious of not overworking the bulletin or special report unless the news justifies breaking into a program. We do follow the hourly CBS Network newscasts with local news if it is warranted. The actual newscasts are handled on the air by regularly assigned news announcers. Actualities by newsmen and people involved in the news are used within the newscast. This, of course, includes our own newsmen as well as telephoned reports from our stringers.

With a limited staff, we can cover first hand many more stories with a combination radio and television reporter. If the story is big enough, naturally we will send reporters to cover radio and television separately. However, we have found that a large majority of the stories can be properly covered by one well trained reporter. If the story warrants, an immediate phone call is placed to the radio editor, and he decides if this should go on the air immediately. A follow-up or in-depth report can be made when the reporter returns to the newsroom.

A stringer setup can make or break an area station news operation. From our standpoint, we maintain stringers in each of the 40 counties served by our basic half milivolt signal. In addition, and this is very important, we maintain almost full time correspondents in Raleigh, Columbia, Chapel Hill and Washington. To illustrate the use of these men, let me give an example of the manner in which they work. If there is a story out of Washington, that has particular importance to North or South Carolina, our correspondent will deal primarily with the Carolina lawmakers involved in the story. In many instances, both CBS and the wire services will have covered the story in some detail. However, the main purpose of the Washington stringer is to get a more in-depth report from the lawmakers or government officials that are directly involved in the story. In most cases, this will involve one of the four North or South Carolina Senators or one of the Congressmen. If necessary, the story may also involve a local stringer or one of our newsmen following up in a particular county or city that has or will play a major part in the story. In many instances, our correspondent will get a story prior to being released to the wire services.

Our stringer setup can work two ways. A stringer can be assigned a story by our news editor, or he or she can call in a story on a speculative basis. From a payment standpoint, they are paid if the story is used on the air. Equipment-wise, we maintain nine two-way radio equipped automobiles, three of which are company owned wagons, and six are personally owned cars. One of the news wagons is equipped with a mobile telephone for use outside the metro area. In the WBT newsroom, the following emergency frequencies are monitored at all times: Charlotte City Police, Mecklenburg County Police, State Highway Patrol, City and County Fire Departments, ambulance services, and airport control tower. Area police and fire officials are provided with a special telephone number "hotline," which is monitored 24 hours a day. Emergency monitoring and radio dispatching on Sunday is done from a duplicate emergency radio setup in the news manager's home.

The WBT Radio desk in the newsroom is equipped with both reel and cartridge recording equipment to take stringer reports, tape network news, City Hall newsroom, lines from master control, and two additional telephone services. This was made possible through a small transistor mixer designed and constructed by one of our engineers. Obviously, we believe very strongly in using as many actualities by our newsmen as possible. We have a "hot mike" line in the newsroom direct to master control, and this is used only when the story warrants it.

Each of our newsmen has special assignments, that he is responsible for on a day by day basis. For example, one man is assigned to City Hall, one man assigned to County government, one man to North Carolina politics, one man to South Carolina politics, one man assigned to entertainment and the arts, etc. Incidentally, the entertainment and arts assignment is handled by our only girl reporter, who does a very fine job. While each of these people is used on general assignments in other areas, it is their responsibility to get to know all the people involved on a close personal basis.

Programming in public affairs has been a part of the WBT operation for decades, but the emergence of a public affairs department separate from the program department occurred in 1962.

It was the success of an unusual radio series that led to the formation of this department which is now charged exclusively with editorial and documentary activities. In 1959 WBT began a weekly commentary called "Radio Moscow" which attracted such widespread attention that it was supplied to commercial and educational stations over the next few years. The daily English broadcasts of the North American Service of Radio Moscow were tape-recorded with the use of special equipment installed at a staff engineer's home outside the city. The most significant commentaries of the week were played in a 15 minute format which included an answering comentary at regular intervals, exposing the uses of propaganda. Extensive files were built on subjects of international affairs and American life by the retired newspaper editor who was hired to prepare the commentaries and edit the tapes. So when WBT was ready to begin editorializing on the air in March, 1962, both the research files and the experienced writer, Mr. Rupert Gillett, were well prepared in experience and background.

The "Radio Moscow" series itself was selected as a national Junior Chamber of Commerce project in 1964 and 1965, and over 50 stations across the country carried it as a syndicated program placed by local Jaycee chapters. In 1961, the series was awarded the top national award for Radio Journalism by Sigma Delta Chi, the journalistic fraternity.

The "bread and butter" of the public affairs function is, of course, the editorials which run five days a week, four times a day. An editorial board composed of eight company officers has the responsibility of approving a corporate opinion on issues of the day ranging from local problems to those of the station, nation and world. Printed copies of the final draft are distributed to a mailing list of 700 interested persons who have asked to receive them, and requests for individual copies sometimes run into the thousands on controversial issues. Invitations to respond are sent out on each editorial, and responses average about one in seven. If the invited person does not respond, appropriate letters are sometimes chosen from the considerable volume of mail that comes in. The editorials are read by Alan Newcomb, the responses by a designated staff member. Newcomb also makes a great many speeches throughout the area and the Southeast on public affairs, serves on a state Governor's Commission and is on the board of a number of local civic institutions.

Undertaking serious editorial comment on genuine issues has been a surprisingly pleasant experience. Naturally, there are critical and even angry responses at times, but the bulk of mail and individual comment has not only been much larger than expected, but has been overwhelmingly favorable. In agreement with our positions or not, the great consensus of expressed opinion has been that of enthusiastic acceptance of radio editorializing, and appreciation for the service it renders the community and the nation. A meticulous concern for the provisions of the Fairness Doctrine has not weakened the station opinions in the public mind, but evoked a consistent flow of good comment about the station's sense of fair play.

Requests for editorials have come in from every state along

the eastern seaboard, and other stations have read them on their own air; so occasionally a few dozen requests will come from Youngstown, Ohio or Red Bank, Montana. An informal committee for cleaning up news stands in a Chicago suburb was started out of suggestions made in a WBT editorial on pornography, and printed copies of editorials have appeared in newspapers and trade press over the eastern half of the country and in the *Congressional Record*. Some school libraries post the editorial on their bulletin boards, civics teachers have used them for class study, and the University of North Carolina is building a permanent file of all WBT editorials since their beginning.

With a staff of three persons, the WBT Public Affairs Department is established as a separate function from WBT News, thus helping to maintain the image of objectivity and straight reporting that has characterized our news department since its beginning. Although newsmen may contribute editorials in areas where they have specialized knowledge, they then go through the same processing and approval as other editorials, and appear on the air as read by the public affairs director, who confines himself to editorials, interviews, documentaries, and panel discussion programs.

The public affairs department made regular contributions to the successful "Project 60" series for several years: A few examples —a liberal-conservative debate between Harry Golden and Dr. Nicholas Nyaradi during the 1964 presidential campaign, and an hour analysis of comparative ideologies in the world today with Charles Vetter, the Public Information Officer for USIA. Public affairs director Alan Newcomb traveled to Europe in 1963 and produced documentary programs about the activities of Radio Free Europe for this series. More recent contributions to the "Target" series included a colorful documentary on a mock political convention which had engaged the attention of the entire city last year. Other WBT radio programs and editorials in public affairs have been awarded three George Washington Honor Medals from the Freedoms Foundaton and the *Radio-TV Mirror* Magazine Gold Medal, in addition to a number of local and regional awards; most recently, the UPI "Best Editorial" award for 1965.

In perspective, the public affairs department has a great deal more to do with shaping the image of the station in the public mind than its limited staff and budget would suggest, and its program contributions provide an additional force of responsible broadcasting to the WBT day. We were fortunate to have won, along with KMOX, in St. Louis, the Mayor's Award for Community Service for the year 1964. This award was presented last May at the U. S. Conference of Mayors, and as you know, is sponsored by the "Broadcast Pioneers."

Along with all stations in the country we do the usual things such as spot announcements for worthwhile causes, etc. You may get some ideas, however, from some of our projects that we feel are a little beyond the average effort. Each year we sponsor, along with a local Jaycee chapter, a Labor Day picnic to promote highway safety. This consists of all day entertainment in one of the local parks, and has drawn from 25,000 to 30,000 people each year we have held this. We recently sponsored an appearance of a demonstration team from the Special Forces Center in Fort Bragg. The Army sent us 40 seasoned Vietnam veterans to participate in these demonstrations and displays over a four day period. Even with rainy weather, the police estimate that the Green Berets drew approximately 40,000 people for this event. We sponsor a "Woman of the Year" award, with nominations sent in by woman's clubs, and this goes to the woman selected by former winners, who has contributed most to the civic, cultural, and religious life of Charlotte and Mecklenburg County. For the past seven years we have sponsored a "Community Pride" award by visiting 8 different communities in our coverage area each year.

With advance preparation, we send a producer, several members of our talent staff, and engineers, to the town and record the most interesting subjects and people from that community. A week or so later this is played back on the air over a period of a week, with no one segment over 3-4 minutes long. At the end of each year an impartial panel of judges select a Community Pride winner, and we present this town with a Community Pride check of $1,000 and a cup for their Chamber of Commerce or City Hall. This presentation is broadcast live over WBT and has been warmly received by the communities in our coverage area. The purpose of this Community Pride Award is an attempt to enhance cooperation between the towns and communities of the

Piedmont Carolinas. We have just completed the second year of sponsoring, along with the Charlotte school system, the Thomas Jefferson High School Convocation Series. This program is for high school and college students throughout the area to hear outstanding people in various fields and professions. The convocation speakers have been; Senator Fulbright, Mark Van Doren, Margaret Mead, Dr. Glenn Seaborg, John Ciardi (ch-ar-di), and Marvin Kalb. We co-sponsor, with the Charlotte Music Club, the live presentation of "The Creation" each Easter, the "Mesiah" each Christmas at Charlotte's Ovens Auditorium. Each year we distribute thousands of up to date clubs lists, calendar of events, and the company sponsors 14 college scholarships each year.

This community involvement of our public affairs is a most important part of our attempt to be a good community citizen. Let me add that while nothing I have discussed here—other than sponsorship of newscasts—is charged for or sold to the public or our clients. But I strongly believe that a good news operation and a strong public and community affairs function can be one of the greatest aids to healthy sales.

4

VERN MUELLER

After graduation from the University of Oregon, Mr. Mueller started his full-time radio career at KPOJ in Portland, Oregon in 1950 as a staff announcer. He became News Editor in 1951 and program director in 1958, a position he holds today.

WE ONCE WON a Peabody Award for public service programming . . . but that was 1951. There have been some changes in our business since then. In that year an orchestra in Studio A was not uncommon. Actors and singers were frequent visitors. The two programs mentioned on the Peabody Plaque were "Career's Unlimited," a 30-minute show in which we discussed teen-age job opportunities with local businessmen, and "Civic Theatre On the Air," live presentation of the current production of our local theatre group. We also did a history of jazz show, with live music by the Castle Jazz Band. There were others. They were fine for the times, but things have changed. In what other business can yesterday's blockbuster be today's bomb?

We live an exciting, competitive, demanding and constantly changing existence, whether we do our day's work in Portland, Oregon; Scottsbluff, Nebraska or Los Angeles, California. The rewards are sometimes far between, but in my 17 years of experience, the real satisfaction has come from working in news and public service.

In looking for an approach for this paper, I reread a speech delivered by the late Edward R. Murrow before the 40th Convention of the National Association of Broadcasters. That was in 1962, the year Mr. Murrow received the Distinguished Service Award of the NAB. In accepting the award he said: "A communications system is totally neutral. It has no conscience, no principle, nor morality. It has only a history. It will broadcast filth or inspiration with equal facility. It will speak the truth as loudly as it will speak a falsehood. It is in sum, no more or no less than the men and women who use it." I repeat the significant thought "it is no more, or no less than the men and women who use it." We in radio broadcasting have a rare opportunity. The machines are easy to come by. The crisis in the industry is finding the men to use the machines to their best advantage. It is my feeling this is particularly true in the area of news and public service. Radio news remains the untapped area of development. Horizons are unlimited. Our heritage is profound.

Radio news really came into its own in the war years. Born of necessity, it has grown in importance until today, when things really go wrong, people turn to their radio to find out why. In the northeast power failure of 1965 it was radio that played the instrumental role in averting public panic. It was the voice of the man on the radio that calmed the fears. He told the public that the blackout was only temporary, that it was not enemy action, that the situation was being investigated and would be remedied at the earliest possible moment. The industry rose to the occasion.

We have all had our local disasters. I trust we all act and serve in a responsible manner. Radio alerts you to impending danger, and when disaster does strike, radio takes the guessing out of what's going on. When the danger is past, radio helps in rebuilding. But whether it's an impending storm, a flood, school closures, a traffic jam, a lost child, a community project or even a lost dog radio is there to serve. I would like to commend the industry for the high degree of cooperation when the chips are down and we have our own trouble. It never ceases to amaze me how we can compete so aggressively during normal times and under other circumstances come to each others aid, whether it be equipment, manpower or just consolation.

In news it takes the right kind of management philosophy, a dedication to doing a job, and then it takes the right man at that news desk—and when you find him, I urge you to hang on to him. He is one of the most valuable men in your organization. He must be versatile, whether the subject is politics, police news, business developments, sports or a half dozen other areas of news coverage. He must have the courage of his convictions. He must be a self-starter, and he must be informed. He must also be trained.

Where do you find him? Go to your university, especially those with a strong radio department. Let them know what you want, not only at this time but as you anticipate inevitable growth and change. Perhaps you can convert one of your local newspaper reporters. By and large, they will have a solid background. You might be able to train a man yourself, but whatever you do, find Mr. Right. Give him the responsibility, supply him with the tools, exercise a reasonable amount of control, and then sit back and enjoy yourself. Like no other part of the business, you'll find that a good news operation can give you more satisfaction than you might expect.

Our news department cannot be considered large, but I do feel we get a lot of mileage. We produce two 35-minute newscasts each weekday, and a 15-minute newscast in the early morning. This is breaking a few broadcast rules—35-minute newscasts just aren't being done, but we have found them successful. These are solid two-voice newscasts filled with actualities and local reporters, not all on the payroll incidentally. Our business expert is with a local brokerage firm, our weathermen are with the United States Weather Bureau, our beach weather and ski reporters are capable volunteers and, of course, we have established contacts at local government offices. These are in addition to the voices of the people making the news from day to day. On a swap beeper basis we have established contacts with many other radio stations on the west coast.

In news, I don't like gimmicks. A little bit goes a long way. One station I visited not too many months ago had absolutely the most exciting news intro I have ever heard. However, it was all puff. The station was automated. There was no newsman on duty. The engineer's first assignment of the day was to use the morning paper, put the news on a cartridge and make a change when the afternoon paper arrived. Another thing that has disturbed me recently is the headline approach to the news.

Turning to one of my favorite subjects, let's discuss editorials which provide a rare opportunity to serve. I urge you to get into the editorial business. Get your feet wet. It's like writing a speech, getting started is the hard part. Our first memo concerning the subject was written in 1955. We did some talking, but somehow we didn't get under way. Once again the right man made the difference. He finally came along—a broadcast major from Washington State College. He joined the news department. We recognized his potential. It had troubled him that so many children and adults were being seriously hurt by walking or running through these big clear glass doors. Investigation revealed the material used was far too often inferior. We suggested he develop an editorial—it was our first, it ran about four minutes.

Now, a couple of hundred editorials later, we have developed the skills necessary to turn out an average of two editorials a week. They run from 60 to 90 seconds; they are delivered by the station manager and are scheduled at least six times in a given day. We do not bury them in the schedule. As a matter of fact, we put strong editorials in our 35-minute morning newscast. Editorials are clearly labeled as such, and responsible opposing viewpoint is given equal time. At this time our editorial board consists of 5 people—the manager, one of our newsmen, the two performers on our talk shows and myself. We meet once a week without exception, and more often when necessary, to discuss subject material, solidify our position and pinpoint assignments. The first step in embarking on an editorial plan, is to put a policy down on paper, with clear guidelines as to purpose and procedure. There are those of you who will say that you will take a position when the time is right. There is subject material in your community, and it is not hard to discover. We steer clear of what I call "evergreen" material. We don't editorialize about fire prevention week, or keeping Oregon green. We do stay local most of the time, and I think this is important. Whatever you do, don't buy an editorial service. This syndicated approach to one of our greatest broadcast challenges leaves everything to be desired. A solid editorial plan presents a rare opportunity for you to serve.

One of the most rewarding broadcast experiences for me in recent years has been the creation and development of two telephone discussion shows on our station. They have created an outlet for the public to voice their concerns about our community and world we live in. We call the evening broadcast "Nightline." It runs from 7:00 to 10:00 P.M. Monday through Saturday, with its counterpart "Dayline" from 11 to noon each weekday morning. Here again the man that sits in the chair is of the utmost importance. In my opinion it is one of the most demanding performing assignments in our business. It takes preparation, intelligence, mental agility and a sense of balance—and from an administrator's viewpoint, it takes direction and control. I would suggest you not embark on a talk show until you feel certain you have the right man.

Frequent meetings are held with our people and, as mentioned before, they sit in on our editorial meetings. Talk programming without control is an invitation to disaster, but a well planned show with direction, professionally performed, can serve the community as effectively as any vehicle I know of. We use guests frequently. We have telephone equipment that enables a guest to participate with the moderator and the public from his office or hotel room, away from the distractions of the studio—in effect, a party line. This has enabled us to get a busy man away from his meeting or convention for an hour or so to participate. We know we have local government leaders listening. They are concerned with the pulse of the public, a public we have given the opportunity to be heard.

On Christmas Day we play sacred and contemporary holiday music, devoting half-hours to various hospitals and rest homes in the area. Messages of inspiration are delivered by administration people to those currently staying at their institutions. We will do production spots for specific causes. These are just a few of the things we do. I'm sure you do similar things and many more. For the record, radio stations and networks donate about $350 million a year to public service projects. Nearly 99% of all homes in the United States are radio equipped. The national average of working radios per U.S. household is four, and brides to be list a radio as one of their ten most wanted items. Radio is unrivaled as America's number one news medium. Radio news serves the public, as do your strong editorial voice, your knowledge of your community needs, and your awareness and confidence in your ability to serve. News and public service. The rewards are more significant than you can imagine. This area of broadcasting has given us our finest heritage, and the horizons remain unlimited.

5

JIM BORMANN

As director of news and public affairs for WCCO, Minneapolis, Mr. Bormann is a veteran newsman. He joined the Columbia Broadcasting System in 1951 after having first started his news career as a cub reporter for the *Milwaukee Journal*. He later worked in Chicago for both news services, United Press International and the Associated Press and was bureau chief of the AP radio division there.

LOCAL NEWS is one of the most important ingredients of the WCCO-Radio success story. We don't call it "local" news, however. Since WCCO is the only Class A clear channel station in our part of the country, our "locality" is a five-state region. And so our local news beat comprises all or parts of five states. When it comes to strictly local news about Minneapolis or St. Paul, we select only those stories that are likely to command region-wide interest.

This is a rather big assignment, covering spot news in an area that spreads across 124 counties. Often the "spot news" that reaches us through the wire service relays is "spotted" with mold by the time it filters into our WCCO News Bureau. We had to find a better way to expedite outside coverage. Beating the wire services on such stories is really the name of the game, because most of the stations that compete with us rely exclusively—or almost exclusively—on their news teletypes as the *only* source of outside news.

So necessity prodded us into searching for a better way to get faster coverage beyond the range covered by our daily run reporters in the Twin Cities. We developed a close working relationship with the Auto Club—the AAA—which has full-time representatives in every community of county seat size throughout the region we serve. They encouraged these people to call WCCO with immediate reports of changing weather and road conditions, and soon this expanded into an expedited correspondence system. These men became the eyes and ears of WCCO, supplying us with eyewitness reports of major news events in their home town—often while the news was happening. They weren't expert reporters, but they did develop a nose for news. And all we needed was the tip that something was happening. We usually followed through with a callback to the sheriff or other official to get the details.

We installed a "direct line" in our news bureau, and the number was given only to these 165 correspondents who could then ring our news bureau without going through the station switchboard. The system has paid off handsomely, both for us and for the AAA. In addition, this crew of unpaid correspondents is supplemented by the voluntary help of hundreds of country newspaper editors. When there's a big story in their home towns, they prefer to call us, rather than see their story in print in a nearby daily. It may be days before they go to press with the story, but when they give it to us, we credit them by name and we mention their paper, and that makes it "their story."

I don't want to leave the impression that such coverage represents the sum-total of news on WCCO. The flow of information from outside correspondents is blended with original coverage by our own staffers. And we often dispatch staffers into the region—and even overseas—to develop regional angles on important general news stories. When I went to the Common Market countries of Europe with a group of Minnesota businessmen, our coverage emphasized business opportunities for Minnesotans. When I visited India, Thailand and Vietnam with Senator Mondale, I reported about the men from our region that I saw in action there. We leave it to our network to cover the "big picture," and I believe CBS does a first rate job on that.

You may be interested in what we've done to match-up our news with news from the network. All-told, news and news-related programming represents about 22% of our total programming on

WCCO. The network share of that portion is less than half. Wherever possible, we try to surround the network newscast with our own regional coverage. There are two reasons: 1) By presenting their news and ours in tandem, so to speak, we offer our listeners a balanced, comprehensive summary of the whole range of news; 2) By opening the period with regional news, then going to general news from CBS, and concluding with regional weather summaries, we manage to bracket the net and give our own WCCO identification to the over-all news package.

This is necessary if we are to maintain our leadership in news and in broadcasting generally. WCCO-Radio enjoys the unique distinction in a 17-station market of gaining and holding more listeners than all other stations combined. This measure of acceptance, which is the greatest for any station in any multiple station market in America, is based to a great extent upon news programming. Our audience flow chart shows a major newscast at the tip of each of the peaks—day and night. And our news audience between 7 and 8 A.M. daily surpasses the audience for *any* television audience in the market.

In a real sense, news on WCCO-Radio provides the pegs from which our entire program structure is suspended. Not only do the immediate adjacencies benefit; the carry-over and the high level of attention throughout the broadcast schedule is largely predicated on our practice of maintaining what we call "news flow." This means that news—spot news—will be heard in *any* program at any time. We don't hold news for newscasts; we let our audience in on news *whenever* it is breaking. Some of our most exciting news coverage comes during entertainment programs.

For instance, while Senator Hubert Humphrey was talking to the folks back home on "Party Line" during the national Democratic convention in Atlantic City, the program was broken by a Net Alert. It was Dan Rather of CBS reporting from the White House that President Johnson was about to call Humphrey and summon him to Washington. This was the first substantial indication that LBJ had, indeed, chosen HHH as his running mate. It was also the first that Humphrey had heard about it. He listened to the bulletin, and then said: "Well, I guess I'll have to say 'goodbye,' and get off the line. A fellow could miss the train this way."

Nothing on the station is so sacred that it can't give way to fast-breaking news. It's this practice of news primacy that accounts for our listeners' reliance on our station for news. When a series of six tornadoes swept through the Twin Cities metropolitan area last May people were sitting in front of their TV sets. It was prime time on TV. But while the TV stations continued their regular schedules, people turned instinctively to their radios and switched to WCCO for a minute-by-minute account of the tornado movements by eye-witnesses. Hundreds of tornado victims whose homes were destroyed wrote later to say: "WCCO Radio saved my life. I took your advice, went to the basement, and the house blew away over my head."

Service like this won all three top national news awards in 1965, but what's more important, it wins listener loyalty. In our book, that's an even higher dividend.

PART TWO

News and Public Service

Modern Radio's Major Role

Small Markets

6. RICHARD JACKSON
   President, WBEC, Pittsfield, Massachusetts

7. JOHN H. LEMME
   General Manager, Radio KLTF, Little Falls, Minnesota

8. JULIAN HAAS
   President, KAGH, Crossett, Arkansas

9. JOHN HURLBUT
   President, WVMC, Mt. Carmel, Illinois

10. GEORGE J. VOLGER
    General Manager, KWPC, Muscatine, Iowa

6

RICHARD JACKSON

Mr. Jackson entered broadcasting in 1948 with WAVE-TV in Louisville, Kentucky. He later joined J. M. Mathes Advertising, New York City as vice president and director of radio and television. In 1961, he became president and owner of WBEC, Pittsfield, Massachusetts.

It is only fair to preface my remarks with the warning that much I say will be in the subjective, rather than objective. This, I think, is of necessity, particularly when trying to come to grips with small market news, for it seems to me there is less similarity between the personality of small markets than there is in larger metropolitan markets. As a case in point, I have been connected with only two small market radio stations. One is a hopefully forgotten venture in the boondocks of the Florida Everglades. If memory serves—and I hope it doesn't—the station carried the call letters of WRIM, and was located in Pahokee, Florida, a thriving metropolis of some 1,500 to 3,000 people on the shores of the world's largest expanse of inland water, Lake Okeechobee. Big news here came with the annual spring flood, but even then, our reports for the most part were heard only by stray alligators most of whom had gotten the word well before our reporters. Our biggest client was the merchant across the street from our studios who sold rain gear to the itinerant laborer who came in to pick the bean crop—and then at season's end bought all the stuff back for 25% of his sale price in time to turn around and sell it for 100% to the next influx of labor. This way he maintained a constant inventory, and supplied the station with a sure spot revenue twice a year.

My second venture is my current one, WBEC, Pittsfield, Massachusetts, and I am happy to report that we have people for an audience instead of alligators, although there is some question in my mind as to how much difference this makes in some areas. There have been moments when I am sure that the alligator population is a bit quicker in paying their bills than the Yankees of western Massachusetts, with whom we currently deal.

Pittsfield is unique and peculiar. We are the hub of beautiful Berkshire County, the most westernmost piece of real estate in the Commonwealth of Massachusetts, a slab of land running north to the Vermont border, south to the Connecticut border, and bounded to the west by New York state. Just 35 miles from Albany, we are nonetheless shielded to a certain degree by mountainous terrain on both sides. We are blessed with the understandable apathy of our big sister stations in the Albany-Troy-Schenectady area, who have little interest or time for Berkshire County news, but who fill the heads of our teenage population with the latest top 40 tunes. And to the east from the Springfield-Holyoke-Chicopee complex comes only restful silence, for the signals do not transcend the line of protecting hills. This then leaves the four Berkshire County stations as sole dispensers of local and regional news, along with the press, the mighty evening *Berkshire Eagle,* and to a lesser extent, the smaller *North Adams Transcript,* who manage to write their headlines from our radio newsbeats. TV is a factor in our market, as it is in most, but here again we are blessed with foreign origination, and no intrusion on local news. By air, only the Capitol City station, and Hartford can be readily received, although these are aided and abetted by the most mature TV cable system in the country who have almost a ⅓ penetration of the Central Berkshire market and do supply one thread of continuity with our state capitol in Boston by offering the programs of WHDH.

WBEC is one of two stations in Pittsfield, a metropolitan market of some 77,000 people (a complex that is 235th in terms of population in the country, but about 15th to 20th in the country in terms of retail sales per family). There is a station north-county serving North Adams, and one serving Great Barrington to the south, but I think it is fair to say that each station is dominant in its own area and is not a factor to its county neighbor—at least as far as news is concerned, for we each make our "big points" in our own small markets. Overall, the county population reaches about 144,000 people, so the proportion of broadcast service to population is amazingly accurate.

But we are a resort area, and our population swells and contracts, although you could almost say we are a four-season resort —for we feature the Tanglewood Music Festival, Jacob's Pillow Dance Festival, summer theatre of note, 25 summer camps, and other delights for the heavy transient trade; we have mature skiing developments for the winter; foliage delights in the fall along with the hunting and fishing; and we have no spring whatsoever.

So, how do we sum up this market for radio news? I think you would have to say that there is an unusually big opportunity for radio in Berkshire County to serve its people with news, for along with one dominant paper, we alone are the only sources for local and state news. Radio's role is perhaps more important in Berkshire County than in most counties throughout the country, and yet we sit within the borders of the defined megalopolis, equal-distance between New York and Boston (150 miles) and only a stone's throw from the capitol of New York state.

Our market, then, is uniquely suited for a good news service. But, what are some of our problems? To start with, I bought WBEC from the *Berkshire Eagle*—which you will recall is that dominant newspaper, and a good one—a prize winner for a city of its size. WBEC was apparently put on the air in 1947 to "protect" the newspaper interests against the predicted growth of broadcasting, and more particularly against the original independent radio station in the Berkshires, our present good competitor whose call letters I shall not mention. But like many newspaper-owned properties, the intent was more defensive than offensive, and the paper jealously guarded its own newsbeats. Hence, its news coverage, written by newspaper staffers was toothless, colorless, restrained, insipid. The other station, therefore, whether it had good or bad news, certainly had better news, and the habit of the Yankee audience solidified around the competitor. This, then, was my problem number one—how to revitalize the WBEC news to capture our share of the audience? A second problem which is common to all broadcasters was one of personnel. How do you get professionals to staff the departments, that you can afford—and, who are willing to work hard enough to cover the area necessary? Three, how do you overcome the extraordinary dependence, that the community has developed, to the local newspaper over too many long years? Releases are given in some cases only to the newspaper, or in advance to the newspaper so that it can favorably compete with radio's immediacy. The newspaper has 42 reporters throughout the county, and WBEC has two full-time newsmen.

Four, how do you get out from under the time-worn provincialism of playing up every obituary (it is the habit in Pittsfield to give these free, and neither hell nor high water can turn this around —to ignore them leaves you wide open)? How also can you upgrade the taste of the community so they will welcome Boston news that affects them on such matters as state taxes, and other legislative actions; how do you overcome the thirst for bent-fender reports, police blotter crap, and the like without losing local following? Five, how do you get the local police to cooperate when they have lived a life-time of catering only to the newspaper except when they need the immediacy of radio?

These are just some of the problems we faced, and to be honest, I can't say that we have licked any one of them completely but—of this I am sure—we have made some strenuous strides. What follows, then, is an outline of our efforts, over some five years, to cope with our responsibility as a community station. We have not always moved ahead as rapidly as we would have liked, but we have always moved. Obviously, we believe that what we are doing is right, and much of our action is applicable to markets other than Pittsfield, so take from it what you will.

We started with the premise that there is no fun or accomplishment in radio if you are not a force in the community, and the only thing to set us aside is a good news and public service approach. Anyone can play a Frank Sinatra record, or talk about the early hits of Kay Starr, before they spin the latest disc.

Obviously, we told the *Eagle,* from whom we purchased the

station that we had no need for the services of their three newspaper reporters who were assigned radio news, because we noted that their copy was newspaper copy, not radio material—and anyway, we figured the chances for taking them out of their rut of newspaper dominance was nil. We patterned our approach on the ABC network with whom we are affiliated (we even used a bit of their identification to lend continuity). This meant frequent beeps or actualities—trying to get the man who made the news to state it on the air, or if he wasn't available, the next best guy who had the insight on the story. We called it "Open Line News," and sold the concept that our mikes were everywhere, and open to pick up the latest news as it was made, and by the guy who made it. For a time we even larded this with some actualities in off-news periods which came over our network line, but which were not being used by ABC in their newscasts. We recorded these and billed them as "Here is a WBEC Open Line Report from Ankhara, Turkey." So well did we do the job that, to this day, people identify any of our shows as "I heard on the open-line . . ." We kept a boxscore of beepers heard on our news, and if it didn't increase with each week, management squawked until it became second nature to our newsmen.

Secondly, we coupled this open-line thrust with an almost indiscriminate policy of picking up community service programs. This we did with remote equipment or lines and included everything from hearings on the local race track in a lonely school tucked in the hills of near-by Hancock (serviced by a local non-Bell telephone company with a president who was always on the golf course), to coronation ceremonies of the local winter carnival queen. We had speeches by conservationists, good government association meetings, political forums, low powered speakers from the MSPCC (that Massachusetts Society for the Prevention of Cruelty to Children), Town Player presidents—in short, anything of reasonable note that smacked of being "public service." This took time, and money for the lines, and I shall never claim that our coverage was always top grade. But it sold the concept that we were interested in the community—which we were and are—and believe it or not, it even made our staid old competitor run a bit faster, and add a few remotes of his own. This too, was good for dignifying the importance and immediacy of radio in the Berkshires.

Frankly, we have become more selective of late in our approach to our beyond studio coverage for three reasons. One, we can now afford to be; two, we get many more requests now as a result of our priming than we could ever fulfill, and three, we can accomplish the same end by getting to the featured speaker ahead of time, taping a highlight of his prepared remarks and setting them in our regular news segments.

As time went on, we adopted the popular "call-in-program-format" which we called "Sound Off" and accomplished it with a seven second delay. This was new to Pittsfield, and exclusive in the area to WBEC, and we received accolades for our brilliance and invention. This, beyond providing entertainment, frequently *made* news as it was closely listened to by City officials who were quick to call up and answer complaints or at least to take soundings on what the great unwashed public had on its collective mind. It is still, after three years, one of the highlights of the broadcast day. We used to have a guy named George doing it, but he is on the road with the Pittsfield Red Sox broadcasts (we do their entire schedule), so we were pleased to put our news director, one Ron Stratton, on the show. For our type of show this is preferable, because if things get slow he can suggest subjects by commenting on the day's news, a subject with which he is obviously familiar.

We recommend the use of a newsman as MC on such a show, for not only can he keep it current and in better perspective, but he is probably best qualified to handle the occasional guest that appears on the show. We made some statewide news with an appearance by Governor Volpe, and have had other big names submit themselves to the whims of the public from time to time. A word of caution on this type of show when it has, as ours does, an overtone of news or current events to it. Be sure to set up good ground rules, for it can quickly get out of hand. We had a frightful go-round on a school superintendency issue which boiled down to a fight on religious differences, and a sticky time with a police pay-raise proposal which brought the police down on our necks. This can be murder in a small city where frequently people can recognize voices even though we do not use a caller's name on the air. Shortly after getting on the air with "Sound Off," we moved into editorials, which has proven more successful than our fondest dreams. These are delivered by me, and researched primarily by me in conjunction with some help from the news department. I waited impatiently for a period of about two years before originating editorials for it takes at least this much time in the Berkshires before the natives would even deign to take a newcomer seriously, and even then it is doubtful. But here we advertised ourself as a "needed second voice" (to the Eagle's editorials). I try to keep as local as I can, feeling much less qualified to tackle a national dilemma, and much less believable.

We are proud of our local sports coverage, which incidentally is one of the best ways to build an audience, but let's just say that we always include scores in our major newscasts in the A.M., or evening, as appropriate, hitting only those with regional or local flavor. For instance, we'll give you the results of the Boston Red Sox in our local news, but you'll have to wait for a sports program to get the complete major league run down. On a local level, we'll rip off all the Eastern League scores (only three, incidentally) leading with the fortunes of our own Pittsfield Red Sox, and there's usually room for the high schools too, or major Babe Ruth League or Little League action.

Handsome dividends can be yours in a small market, by doing the obvious, which I would assume that we are all doing—remotes on Fire Prevention Week, featuring fire fighters and maybe sponsored by the local insurance agents, inclusion of auto license deadline reminders, or safe driving warnings as closing news fillers. Spend some time romancing your local Social Security office, and let them handle question-and-answer programmettes, ditto with your local member of the cloth, police departments, school officials, and be sure to leave some time for your Congressman and Senator to make a weekly report on tape. Encourage your staff to enter into community activities so you'll be in on the know for plans for a UCS, Good Government Association, or church function—you can remind them not to hand all the news to the local press—and keep reminding your entire staff from janitor to general manager to pass on any news that they pick up, or see in the making, because this adds an extra dimension to your tiny news staff. For somewhere, tucked in amongst the obvious, you're going to run on to a good story from time to time that will make it all worthwhile, even while you're making friends in the meantime.

7

JOHN H. LEMME

Born in Duluth, Minnesota where he attended public schools and Duluth Junior College, Mr. Lemme graduated from the University of Minnesota Law School in 1952. He became owner and president of Radio Station KLTF, Little Falls, Minnesota that same year. A member of the board of directors of the Minnesota Power and Light Company, Mr. Lemme is also vice president and board chairman of Crestline Products, Inc. He has served as a member of the board of directors of the National Association of Broadcasters and the Minnesota Broadcasters Association. He is currently serving in the state legislature of Minnesota.

I WOULD LIKE TO give you my impression of small market news and how it can be improved economically and still effectively. In this context I think it is necessary to ask some very basic questions. Does small market news differ from large market news? If so, in what respect? How can a small market station, many times an independent, offer the quality of service, depth and detail that is part and parcel of a good news operation?

Let us start by looking at the typical small market news operation—understaffed, a robot in the back room that sends copy on yellow or white paper to such an extent that "rip and read" has replaced "Stop and Think" in the nomenclature of the so-called news department of the typical station. Imagination and the application of the principle of methodology have been largely subverted to a similarity that can only serve to damage the most powerful arm of the small market station, news, which does not mean never-ending worn sound, but should reflect a new empire of wide stimulus.

Reliability, credibility and respect do not accrue to the station that fails to discharge its stewardship to the public through diligence. Perserverance is the extra effort that sets apart the innovator from the imitator.

It is my belief that news does not differ between small market and large market insofar as substance is concerned . . . the goal is the same. Insofar as content is concerned, it becomes a matter of serving the needs of the market. Our station believes that a good news operation does not have to have a large budget to accomplish the goal, but does require a concentration on local and area coverage. National and international news is important also, but we do not use a bulletin to tell our listener of a train wreck in Istanbul, or a New Zealand ship that has run aground off the coast of Formosa. Our coverage of national and international news must be left to the imagination of the guy who is hiding in the wire service machine and does not provide us with anything different than any other radio station in the United States. Because we are an independent station we must do something different in an attempt to capture the attention and loyalty of our audience when it comes to news.

There is no place in our news format for gimmicks, showmanship or anything other than factual informative news reporting. The news we attempt to provide for our audience is designed to give them something they can get nowhere else, or at least in greater depth and detail than anywhere else. In this area we feel we are doing a good job and find that more and more people look to us for not only the first story but the most knowledgeable story. We like to believe that a great deal of the respect we have earned is due to our lack of gimmicks and our concentration on factual, informative reporting. When our bulletin intro is used, it means something of startling import has happened on the national or international scene, a matter of wide concern on the regional scene, or a tragedy on the local scene. I for one do not agree with those stations who spend most of their time and budget on promotion and gimmicks that sacrifice the news that is important. Those who would rather blow their own horn than listen to the Marine Band, serve to damage the cause of good radio.

The telephone and tape recorder aptly demonstrate the immediacy and impact that is radio's alone. No other medium can provide direct, on-the-scene reports as quickly, factually and with greater drama than radio. When certain juvenile activities in our area became a matter of widespread public concern, we asked the Juvenile Court judge to appear on the air and answer questions called or sent in by listeners. At the same time, the Juvenile judge had an opportunity to explain to the public some of the policies and thinking that is involved in the treatment of juveniles brought before his court. The public was vitally concerned as to the reasoning involved in decisions of Juvenile Courts that dealt with either publishing or not publishing the names of juvenile offenders. We took our tape recorder to the main intersection of our town and asked passersby whether they thought the names of juvenile offenders should be published. We took the replies as they were given and ran them on the news. We believe news is people and feel that this type of report, with the sound of our city in the background, gives depth, meaning and immediacy to our newscast.

With a small staff it is not possible to send out a horde of reporters to cover every event that takes place, and yet a staff that is aware of and concerned with news of our community and area will keep on top of events. Once again, the cooperation of people in our area is of utmost necessity in our type of operation, lending further support to the premise that every radio station should be a community leader. Our staff includes people who have served as president of the Chamber of Commerce, Chamber Committees, president of the Jaycees, president of the Baseball Club, leaders and directors of service clubs, church groups, active participation in and leadership of the American Legion, Knights of Columbus, Masonic Lodge, and other social groups. Our station is people, and people provide the leadership that we feel is so necessary for our image. We spearhead and provide the community leadership that takes radio from the jukebox state to a respect that is earned and deserved. It does not come easily. It must be earned and earnings, monetary or real, cannot be separated from work. Certainly, miracles cannot be expected overnight, for this is a continuing and never ceasing goal where the yardstick of achievement should be never reached but always raised.

Of necessity, we must rely on others to assist us in gathering our news. I do not wish to convey the thought that we take what they provide, but it does help to have them respect your staff and your station.

In 1965, when our sheriff and his chief deputy were shot and killed, it was our station that started a memorial fund for the families of the slain law enforcement officers. We also sponsored a variety show with proceeds to go to the fund and due to the widespread feeling generated by the slayings, the talent we obtained was the finest available in our entire area. The packed High School auditorium witnessed a show that by acclamation was hailed as the finest presentation of local talent that had ever been seen in our community. Even our newspaper mentioned the show and the fact that over $6,000 was turned over to the families of the slain men.

Our law enforcement people, police, sheriff and constables, fire department, highway patrol and hospitals all offer good cooperation to us and yet we do have the constant struggle between what we feel is news and what the others feel is not our business or the public's business. In this area we have become involved in areas of disagreement. By maintaining our standards and insistence on fair and impartial news that *we* make a decision on and not the agency that reports it, we have been able to reach a reasonable accord. We now have in the planning stage a gathering of law enforcement people in our area at which time we hope to conduct a seminar that looks at their problems and ours in the belief that such an exchange of ideas and viewpoints will result in a greater understanding between our differing problems. We will serve as hosts and representatives of these agencies will be invited as well as station personnel.

The telephone and tape recorder, as mentioned earlier, are probably the most underestimated facilities at the disposal of a station. If news is people and your news department is nothing more than one or two men trying to fill in with news as well as selling, anouncing or whatever else they are required to do, what greater expenditure is required to use the voices of people who make the news rather than your own? When there is a report from Juvenile Court, the station can state the story in the voice of its regular news announcer, but how much better does it sound to have a report from the Morrison County Probation and Parole Officer of activities in Juvenile Court? He knows his business, we help by suggesting how he write the story. The same situation can work with many others, including the chief of police, fire chief, organization heads and the like. We help them with the story, they like to hear their voices and we feel it gives a newscast greater immediacy and more vivid portrayal of people—people who are involved. It is simple to use the telephone to record such stories and it takes no longer than it does to write it up yourself. We record City Council meetings, use excerpts to supplement our coverage and give the same impact of people who are involved. We like it, the people who speak on radio like it, the public likes it, and no other medium can duplicate the sense and spirit of news involved in such reporting.

It is true a limited budget station cannot go directly to Saigon for a report on Vietnam, to the White House for a Presidential news conference, or if there is another one to the scene of a Gemini shot, but you can go across the street and this is the area you serve and is important. Certainly, there is no substitute for expanding these ideas into a regional and national picture, if possible, but the limited budget station can do much that no one else can do in the area of news. Your personnel must know the area they serve, must be knowledgeable and skilled in news and although there is no substitute for experience in this area it is possible to develop these skills if the basic material is present.

Much of what I have said in this paper has been intertwined with the basic premise of a respect and admiration for your station that is given only when it is earned. The method of doing this may differ from station to station and market to market, yet there is one subject that in my opinion is so important in the development of this respect that I cannot finish without referring to it. The middle road, the white line down the center of the highway or the top strand in the middle of a barbed wire fence are not areas where you will ever build the respect and leadership you want or the reputation for fair, factual and meaningful news that can elevate radio to its rightful position. The mantle of community leadership goes beyond involvement in the community, it entails and must be coupled with station leadership, also. Too many times the station that has its personnel involved in community life feels that this is all that is necessary. It will do the job. To those I must respectfully dissent. This is not enough. How does this alone give image to your station except that you have a bunch of nice guys working there? Does it mean they know what they are doing in quest of station business? Do they know anything about how to run a radio station?

It is my firm and dedicated belief that only when station leadership is coupled with community leadership can news reflect never ending wide stimulus. How do you do it? What does it take? My answer is one word, *editorialize*. The station that editorializes gives depth, clarity and thought to everything it does. It also gives purpose and meaning for our responsibility to serve in the public interest encompasses the responsibility to speak out on issues of the day. Whether it be reapportionment in Minnesota, colored oleo in Wisconsin, farm prices in Iowa, the tax base in North Dakota or whatever your problem might be, you will find a drastic change in the way your public looks at you if you speak out. Closer to home are the matters of teachers' salaries in your district, city council actions, farm organizations, juveniles, police, sheriff's office, local traffic problems, taxes and spending, and the untold thousands of subjects that people today are concerned with.

It is not easy. You are bound to offend some people. It does mean work. But you will earn respect for everything you do on your station. We do not ask that everyone agree with our position. The right to dissent is basic to our society and our way of life. All we ask is that people use what has been given to them and *think*. In thinking, they will respect you, admire you and listen to you. Editorials have no part of regular news broadcasting. Yet, while fulfilling one of your obligations to the public you serve, you will also fulfill something else—a greater measure of success for your station.

The small market station cannot go to Saigon but it can go across the street; it can stimulate the minds of the people it serves and, after all, news is people. How you serve them is up to you. Your service to them also creates the image of radio everywhere.

We in radio, large market and small, have a vital part to play in our civilization. It involves more than record albums and gimmicks. In the words of Ralph Waldo Emerson, "The true test of civilization is, not the census, nor the size of the cities, nor the crops, but the kind of man that the country turns out." The mantle of leadership is ours in radio. We must pick it up and wear it.

8

JULIAN HAAS

Mr. Haas started in radio as a salesman at KARK, Little Rock in January, 1941. He served as commercial manager from 1945 until he became owner of KAGH, Crossett, Arkansas, October 1, 1952. Having served two terms as a member of the board of directors of the National Association of Broadcasters, Mr. Haas is currently serving as a member of the NAB Small Market Committee. He was one of the original members of the Arkansas Broadcasters Association, having served in every capacity including the presidency in 1961.

CROSSETT IS eight miles north of the Louisiana line in the extreme southeastern tip of Arkansas. It is located on U. S. Highway 82, 45 miles east of El Dorado, Arkansas, and 80 miles west of Greenville, Mississippi. The latest census shows a city population of about 5,300 persons; an additional 5,000 to 6,000 persons live within the school district. Hamburg, the county seat, 15 miles distant, has a population of about 2,500 persons . . . county population about 27,000.

Prior to 1946 the Crossett Company owned every square inch of Crossett except the post office building, and the town was built solely for the employees. Since that day 20 years ago when the company-owned Commissary, that sold everythig from bassinets to coffins, was closed, the philosophy of the company-owned town passed on. They've shoved back the pines a lot further, but there are still hundreds and hundreds of square miles of virgin forests owned by the Crossett Company's successor, the Georgia Pacific Corporation. This corporation, incidentally, built the first plywood plant in the South. Georgia Pacific utilizes every particle of the tree except the leaves and the roots in products made in Crossett.

KAGH is a sunrise-sunset operation. On the hour, except 7 A.M., we have combined news and sportscasts. We have a complete weather summary at 7:45 A.M. and 4:45 P.M. Besides the full 15-minute summary at 7 A.M., we have another at 12:30. In many instances, with lack of a startling lead, we start the newscast with the temperature and the immediate forecast. In fact, the weather is a "must" in every newscast and we have a board posted with the last year's hi-lo and precipitation in front of the announcer. We have a late afternoon sportscast at 5:15.

We do not have a full time newsman. We follow the five-minute, every hour on the hour newscasts Sundays, but every afternoon we place heavy emphasis on the sport results. During the baseball season we give the line scores of the preceding day and night games at half hour intervals starting at 6 A.M. None of the three morning newspapers delivered in Crossett from out of town can say the same! That's a "must" for small—even large stations these days of night ball.

Our announcers use their own judgment if a story warrants a bulletin or a news check. We have taped openings and closings for them in order to allow the necessary brief pause before the announcer actually reads the news item! Stories of local and regional origination, plus obituaries, are broadcast in the next available newscasts and left for the next announcer to use with a new lead or repetition "as is."

Our staff is small—a program-traffic director and three announcers. In writing stories they are instructed to keep it brief; never go into details; quote someone in authority; and never make it appear KAGH is a judge, prosecuting or defense attorney. Above all, we strive to get the names correctly, including if possible the middle initial, and all the facts. We never *double time* like 6 A.M. this morning—8 P.M. tonight.

Few stories exceed two or three paragraphs. We leave the details to the weekly newspaper. Or, as my first city editor told me: "Give me the 'guts,' you keep the rest yourself." Incidentally, that same city editor, on my first assignment as a "cub reporter," had me walk 12 blocks on a hot day back to a store where I had gone on a

"B.O.M."—business office must—to get the first name and initial of the person I had interviewed. That was a long-lasting lesson.

And as the late Mr. Hearst used to say: "It's okay to pick up a story but you'd better check your facts, and improve on it." When we go on the air before 6:30 A.M., the announcer gets a taped report of overnight police and fire activities, which we play back about 6:20. True, it's "corn" doing "corn," but our listeners like it and it affords us leads for later stories.

The basic thinking behind our local stories is that the two TV stations, easily accessible to our listeners, can't give 'em the weather—the joys and sorrows of our community—the Kiwanians are going to have a pancake supper tomorrow night and you can eat all you want for a buck—the boy down the street is serving with the engineers in Vietnam—my own son is aboard the carrier "Intrepid" as it picked up the Gemini space fliers—the mobile X-ray unit is in town—High School band concert tomorrow afternoon. These announcements are dutifully noted in our newscasts in just about 10 seconds. But that 10 seconds, *remember,* appeared on radio's *front page.* Can you imagine where the two-line item appeared in the weekly newspaper? I'll tell you. Between the rutabago and the Preparation "H" ad!

Obtaining local news is not only interesting but frustrating, and requires real ingenuity—especially, as the county seat is 15 miles away, and it's hard to locate the sheriff and state highway patrolman. That compounds your problem but that's where ingenuity and the telephone enters. We have learned to call the coroner or his assistant at the funeral home. On many occasions when we can localize the story we'll call nearby residents for their knowledge. It's strictly a case of playing it by ear. Trying to set up a set of rules to follow, in our market anyway is impossible and impractical. However, we use a story only when we are sure of the facts and the true identity of the parties involved. New leads are added if necessary but in the main our original stories stand up.

When we hear a siren, we get with it!! And we never ask how do you like the weather or is business good—but "What's new?" You'd be suprised how many productive news leads you get that way. We have no station wagon emblazoned with our call letters. We have a "beeper" at the station and a small portable recorder which adequately serves our purpose. After the stock market opens, we include a short story in each newscast. We give three closing prices of stocks of area interest on the final newscasts of the day.

Inasmuch as we go off the air as early as 5 P.M. some months, many stories are written after that time. Usually, we write them and take them to the station for early morning broadcast. And, ironically enough, sometimes we kill them for ourselves because, if they are newsworthy, we phone them to the Little Rock AP Bureau—and sure enough they pop back at us on the late evening TV news. Incidentally, during the past 14 months the AP utilized 65 stories phoned in by our station. Many made the national news.

I believe you share with me in two frustrating efforts to try and obtain the news. First, ambulance drivers are interested in getting their patients to the hospital or morgue. Secondly, they are interested in whom they charge for the service. Nurses and other hospital officials sometimes make you feel like a banker that's just poisoned the well at the old folks home. That's why we depend so much on the telephone. Our bellweather news is naturally called "Hometown News," 12:15 Mondays through Fridays. Some have called it a "womb-to-the-tomb" narration. Actually, only a Boswell could catch the conversational riches, the daily cradle roll, obituaries, bridal showers (two announcements to a customer), revivals (one announcement to a customer), track meet this afternoon, mobile X-ray units in town, Mayor Carter seeks re-election, city council actions and on and on and on. Occasionally, we use taped interviews with newsmakers themselves, like St. Patrick's Day we interviewed the only native-born Irishman in town. It is as the name implies, "Hometown News."

Here are a few things we do: We will take second, third, or even fourth carbons of a local handout, but we will not pick it up by request from the local newspaper. By the same token, we do not pick up newspaper stories without verification because in many instances we'd have to correct them. We whittle down all handouts from the schools, industrial groups and other organizations. We will not observe timed releases issued primarily for newspaper use. Our answer is the next time you have an emergency we'll hold it up till the newspaper comes out. When we secure material marked "press release," we advise the sender there are four presses in Crossett—one at each of the of the two laundries, the Bemis Bag plant and one at the weekly newspaper—that, in our business we use microphones and the live spoken word.

When we can't get an authoritative story, we use an announcement. Recently we quieted down parents when a student died from spinal meningitis, by using an announcement from the school superintendent. In the event of a suicide, we use that fact in only one story. We look, too, for the light and bright side of a yarn —like the day state police threw up a roadblock. The number of arrests and warnings were routine, but the fact two bootleggers were caught as they tried to get away was the story. The AP used it!

We exercise extreme caution in the usage of words such as rape, sodomy, carnal abuse. If necessary, we kill the story entirely. However, a little editing and use of the words "criminal assault" instead of rape doesn't make a youngster ask "What does that word mean?"

We editorialize occasionally. We appreciate the privilege but, to do so honestly and without fear of libel, we would have to have a fulltime, qualified newsman and a stand-by attorney.

The basic theory about small or even large-town coverage is an adage I read many many years ago when I broke into the news business. It goes like this: "A dog fight on the courthouse square is a heluva lot more news than a revolution in Central America." Times have changed, but I still think a new industry coming to town or a retired banker 75 years old shooting his age on 18 holes on the local golf course make mighty interesting listening.

Today, more than ever, gathering, writing and reporting local news is a frustrating but rewarding business. It's a great way, I can assure you, to stay young! The networks have their Huntleys, Brinkleys, Paul Harveys, Cedric Fosters and Walter Cronkites. But . . . radio news is the small town's day-by-day, hour-by-hour information center. It is the right now answer to "what's new?"

9

JOHN H. HURLBUT

Mr. Hurlbut is president and general manager of WVMC-Radio, Mt. Carmel, Illinois. Additionally, he is publisher of one daily and two weekly newspapers. He also heads a CATV company, Wabash Cablevision. Mr. Hurlbut has served in various capacities with Time & Life Inc. and Peters, Griffin and Woodward, station representative. A native of upstate New York, he attended Syracuse, University.

SAY WHAT YOU want to about small market radio but, frankly, this is real, down-to-earth radio. And it wasn't until those big 50 kw broadcasters adapted some of our tactics that they started coming out of the doldrums. I can't think of anything sillier than this super power bit because, really, even the 50 kw's are programming for a small area, too. I doubt if anyone in Georgia or Florida gives a damn about traffic on the Lake Shore drive in Chicago.

We live in a day and age of computers, charts and graphs. Statistics seem to occupy us at times, but I'm told it is mighty risky for a broadcaster to use statistics these days. Even those in Congress have been appropriating money based on information from samples thinner and shakier than Don Knotts, yet they have the gall to yell at us and our research. Besides that, in Mt. Carmel a Pulse is something you feel; a Hooper is a fella who yells Amen at a Holy Rollers Convention; and Nielsen? Well when someone gets one of their diaries they call me up and ask me how to use it.

I propose to get into the spirit of a little statistics, and when you get so involved, you wind up with graphs, charts and curves which are supposed to prove something. I want to prove the game of follow the leader with curves.

There is the Bellmont Curve leading into Mt. Carmel and it is a real-time screamer. As the teenagers say, "You often hear the Voice of Firestone" on this one. It is in connection with the Bellmont Curve that I want to show what a radio station can do to move and motivate its listeners and get results. Three years ago, four women were journeying west on Highway 15 which goes from Mt. Carmel to East St. Louis. It was a sunny Sunday morning, one of those pretty June days. Seven miles west of our city is the curve. The Bellmont Curve lies at the bottom of a slight grade. Three years ago, and for 30 years prior to this date, there had been a standard warning sign, the kind of sign that you and I just about ignore everywhere we drive. Anyway, these four women approached the curve too fast, and being on a downgrade, their car was taken over by a combination of gravity and intertia. It went out of control, went off the curve, turned over in a cornfield, killing the driver and seriously injuring her three passengers. This wasn't the first death on the Bellmont Curve. But we at WVMC (this ownership now having been in the market about 18 months) and after considerable inquiry, learned that this situation had nagged and annoyed our area for a generation.

WVMC began editorializing. Three days later I received a *form* letter from the District Highway Engineer with the location filled in the appropriate blanks, and still another blank area filled in with a vague promise that the highway would be re-routed in 1968 or 1969. No mention was made about the signs we asked for. We then scheduled a new and stronger editorial five times a day. What happened? Within 72 hours I had a personal letter from the District Highway Engineer. This, I assure you was not a form letter. In so many words, it said, get off my back, we're going to do something. The letter was one and one half pages in length, with carbons to his boss and even the Governor.

Currently, this is positively one of the best marked curves in the State of Illinois. The signs, one on each side of the road, have flashing lights! The State had to get easements to string the wire for those lights! And finally, there is the sign right smack in the middle of the curve. Only a blind, drunken village idiot could miss these warnings. We have not had a fatality since on this curve. One overloaded truck did tip over. That's all. For weeks after this, people were thanking us for fixing their curve.

This is but one illustration of what a radio station can do to get people motivated, to get them to act, and to get results. How many lives have been saved? At least three, maybe more. How much property damage has been prevented? You can use your imagination.

One month after we took over WVMC, fire gutted the major portion of the Mt. Carmel High School building. The walls were left standing and that is about all you could say. But some of the more substantial people in our town were all for rebuilding within those fire-weakened walls. After all, that school was put up when builders really knew how to build. The structure was good enough for them, and it should be good enough for this generation of kids. Well, we flew in the face of that one and right smack up against some of our better-heeled sponsors. The new Mt. Carmel High School has a new building. There are older annexes in the background. And this building was a result of some steady radio editorializing and campaigning for this much needed new school. We didn't lose an ounce of business, but being new in the market, I wondered if we would. We have a plaque from the Board of Education commending us for our meritorious service in pushing the bond issue which so many said would be defeated. But we are more proud of the new school than the award.

Still on the subject of education, within another year or two it was evident that our public junior college, established in 1960, had outgrown the old buildings in which it was housed. We needed a new junior college building. But there was much chatter around town about taxes and no more building. WVMC got behind this project. I am shortening the story in the interest of space, but we had special programs about the opportunity represented by junior colleges. A number of us formed the Wabash Valley College Foundation and purchased 120 acres of ground. The School District bought 10 acres from us, and when we have the mortgage paid off on the other 110 acres, we'll present the balance of the land to the District. You see, we didn't have enough bonding power or money to go whole hog through District funds. Again WVMC Radio has backed to the hilt the College and the Foundation.

I could cite more examples where we have used our radio station to motivate and lead. At that time we were competing with a newspaper which didn't editorialize, didn't get involved in anything controversial. This paper I bought, incidentally.

In 1963 we ran a series on teenage drinking. Some of the better families were involved. Our editorial series became part of the official minutes of both the City Council and the Board of Education. Within a week, the source of illegal booze was dried up. There was a cross burned on my front lawn by some disgruntled bootleggers. Thanks to our searchlight on the issue, these bootleggers were run out of town. I did have an anxious moment when one of our advertisers, whose son had been tippling, called me in to talk about his advertising. I held my ground, because I knew he really didn't want to talk about advertising. He admitted his wife had given him a little hell concerning junior and our editorial series on these teen drinking parties. And he finally admitted that a station which could raise that much ruckus ought to be able to influence people for his services. We didn't lose the account.

Are you a community leader? Does your station move and motivate? Unfortunately, too many broadcasters choose to be followers, not leaders. They have an inferiority complex about the print media when it comes to influence and power in their home towns. Just watch in which direction the politicians head when they want something done. Do they go to your office? Or do they head for the nearest publisher's office? We have to admit that in too many instances they head for the newspaper publisher's office. How come? Force of habit, partly. Another reason is this. For many years, radio broadcasters rode that network line and considered themselves entertainers pure and simple. Only since the advent of television has radio really emerged as a journalistic force. How much more news and special events coverage are there on radio today compared to the 1930's and 1940's?

One exception, if you please. The late President Franklin D. Roosevelt discovered the secret of radio success with his fireside chats. I say that it was these chats that got him elected and elected and elected. Even so, that intimacy didn't translate to the average broadcaster until many years later. And I say again, it was small market radio that pointed the way to radio's very real power today. It had to influence people with no network to help it program.

Much fiction has been written about the crusading newspaperman. We even had one program on radio about Steve Wilson of the "Illustrated Press" and his side kick, Lorelei Kilburn. We, with our entertainment medium, carried that propaganda about the influence of the Press—the concept that it was the crusading editor who got things done. So newspapers have carried the image of community leadership. We even carried a program called the "Big Story" on radio—documentation of reporters who got things done. How come no one wrote a radio program series about radio reporters? Or weren't there any?

But this picture of the crusading editor and the crusading newspaper is getting more and more tarnished, because fewer and fewer publishers care to stick their necks out. Most are getting old and fat, and have so many financial and union problems that they aren't about to be bothered with the old and increasingly fictionalized role of the crusading newspaperman. These very publishers keep yelling at broadcasting about being influenced by its sponsors, because they are so fearful of their advertisers. No wonder they hurl the charge. It is a natural one to make because of their own fears.

Yes, I am a newspaper publisher. And I go to newspaper conventions. I assure you that there is a distinct contrast between broadcast meetings and some of these print conventions. At broadcast meetings the discussion is about new ideas and exciting ways of using the broadcast media to meet the challenges of an ever changing society. But at most newspaper workshops and conventions, one gets the impression that too many of these old fogies want to fight progress, want to preserve the status quo, and somehow move things back to the good old days of 30 years ago. I just say that this complacency and preoccupation with the past which exists in too many newspaper complexes is a great opportunity for the alert radio broadcaster. The crusading newspaper today is more myth than fact. Radio can, does and will fill this void of community leadership. That is, if we broadcasers want to flex our muscles.

My county has one newspaper. I publish it. *The Mt. Carmel Daily Republican Register* comes out once a day, five days a week.

From Friday afternoon to Monday afternoon, radio is positively the only source of local news! One Memorial Day weekend, we were without a Monday newspaper. We only published four days that week! And we come out at 2:30 or 3 o'clock, depending on the editorial problems and the mood of the pressman. Our carrier boys aim at the front door after school and that's it. But our radio station publishes every minute from 6 A.M. until local sunset and it's within earshot. Our aim is a hell of a lot better than some of my carrier boys!

Some of you feel that the fairness doctrine is a deterrent to being powerful and influential—to getting into the local issues. Unless the fairness doctrine gets more specific and more confining, it is no deterrent! Of course newspapers don't have to be fair in the same sense we think we do, but this is the very factor debilitating their influence. It is significant, for example, that the great *Chicago Tribune,* so commercially successful, hasn't influenced many elections, if any, in recent years.

If a radio station wants to grow, it should learn how to move and motivate its community—not just in getting ratings, but in getting action, in becoming a power. It must latch onto those needs and issues which present themselves and it should get cracking. I say that a small city or middle city or big city radio station need never, never, *never* take a back seat to the newspaper in taking this action. And if you get peppery enough, you'll get the ratings. You see, you can get your listeners' attention so much more than does your newspaper. You publish every minute of the day. And when you publish every minute of the day, you deliver your message in the myriad places where the transistor has taken radio. You have an unrivaled opportunity. And what newspaper, what TV station could duplicate the experience of the astronauts describing the angry alligator in space, which you heard on radio?

It is my theory that the station which influences in the important issues of its community is the station that will wind up with the bulk of the business. Power, properly used, attracts attention. It also attracts money. Even your banker will respect you more! When you motivate your city, when you stimulate your city, you help it grow. And a growing economic strength goes right into your bank account.

In closing, I just ask you this question. Do you really know how powerful you could be in your town? Do you realize what you can accomplish if you just exercise those muscles? Even 250 watts worth can walk circles around a press that just runs once a day. But it means community involvement, community interest and hard work.

10

GEORGE J. VOLGER

Mr. Volger established KWPC AM and FM, Muscatine, Iowa, where he is owner and manager, in 1947. He has served on the original NAB Code Committee and the FM and Freedom of Information Committees. He is a graduate of the University of Iowa and holds a master's degree from the University of Southern California.

TWENTY-FIVE years ago a radio newsman had an exhilarating dream. Practically all homes and automobiles would be radio equipped. A small, portable receiver could literally be with you anywhere. For the newsman, a small lightweight recorder, operating on batteries, would be designed by some genius. Easily portable transmitting equipment would allow him to roam the area for news and feature programs. News actualities from around the world would be available to stations from Muscatine to McMinnville. More and more communities would have their own radio news center. Certainly such events would place radio news well above all competition. With such flexibility to produce news, and such a possibility of exposure, other media might as well prepare for the final blessing.

These dreams did come to pass, but with a few nightmares mixed in. In 1940 there were 765 AM stations; there are now over 4,000. FM outlets have grown from 15 to almost 1,500. Radio receiver growth exceeds all rabbit stories. A population of 195 million is served by 242 million radios—receivers outnumbering people by

47 million! *Ninety-eight per cent* of homes have radios. There are 60 million sets in automobiles, 10 million in public places!

The newsman's tools exceed his finest hopes: beeper phones, low cost, excellent tape recorders, cartridge equipment, expanded wire and audio facilities, WATS, economical portable remote transmitters. With such facilities, why would an energetic, imaginative newsman turn his talents to the slower-paced print media?

"But newspapers feel the competition of broadcast news—they're certainly on the decrease," says a dissenting voice. True, daily newspapers, numbering over 2,000 in 1920, dropped to 1,878 in 1940, and now are at about the 1,750 figure. But circulation in daily newspapers over the last 20 years has gone up from 48 to over 60 million. At least 75 Florida communities have local newspapers where none existed ten years ago. Los Angeles suburbs have 28 suburban dailies, 150 weeklies, and over 100 shopping guides.

Just where and how can radio improve its performance? With our unlimited potential exposure, we cannot be satisfied with a total tune-in of 25-30% between 6 and 9 A.M., less than 20% by mid-day, and 15-18% between 4 and 7 P.M. (Figures compiled by Sindlinger & Co. for RAB, 1964)

What an opportunity we have! In the 1,480 communities with only one radio station, there is essentially only *one* local daily newspaper. Many have *no* daily newspaper. One southern newspaper found 18,000 families in its county that didn't *read* either a morning or evening newspaper. A Kansas paper found 14,000 families not reading a newspaper. A midwest publication estimates 25,000 families do not read a daily paper in its home county. (Wm. Jardine, *Minneapolis Star & Tribune* in *Iowa Publisher,* April 1966)

We wanted to know how listeners regarded our news and programs. A few dollars invested in a simple mimeographed survey with an AP recording of 1965 news highlights for those who answered, gave us a 75% return with extremely valuable information. Listeners told us to check local name pronunciation more carefully, do a better job of re-write, give more detail on obituaries, expand our news contacts, and change the delivery of one announcer. As a manager you may have realized these points, but coming from the listener, it has much more impact. The study also showed the average home surveyed had 4.9 radios, and that our FM saturation was 80%. Another plus: such a survey should fit well into your license renewal forms for the Commission in determining program needs.

Newsmen today should be active with the beep phone and tape recorder. Instead of talking with the city engineer in his office about a street project, perhaps he can record it on the construction site with sound of equipment in the background—or, interview the grain company manager about increase in shipments at the loading dock. Too many of us have forgotten that radio is *sound*.

In addition to the news summaries and features, there is a wealth of separate datelined stories from wire services, most of which are discarded immediately into an overflowing waste basket. A little planning can integrate these stories, and keep our newscasts from sounding like the one a few channels away.

Networks are providing local stations with actualities from around the globe, in addition to regular news feeds. UPI is providing an audio service to small stations not available previously in most areas. As an example of what can be done with network cooperation, a group of Mutual outlets in Iowa has been able to work out a plan whereby a 12-station Iowa Radio Network has been set up, utilizing the network lines for regional news, farm programs and features, when not needed for network commitments.

In addition to spot news, are we making full use of remote units for special saleable features? The opening of a new art gallery or museum, high school graduations, golf tournaments, Soap Box Derbies, Home Shows, are a few of the possibilities. Many times industries and professional people are anxious to sponsor—adding up to "new money" for the sales department. Our requests for time availabilities from local and national advertisers point up their desire to be adjacent to or within newscasts. They know what people want from radio. But do we, as station managers, fully realize it? In a small market there is no other segment of our service which so typifies the character of our operation.

A station manager might well take a close look at the hour-to-hour scheduling of his news operation. If he has only one man, this person may be so tied down preparing frequent on-the-air assignments he has no time to dig out new material by phone and personal contact and certainly does not have the time for the type of investigative reporting which must be done if we are to build the stature of radio journalism. The most ear-catching electronic gimmick doesn't replace news. It just emphasizes the inadequacy of the reporting.

Local, regional and national governmental offices are dry news sources on week-ends. A good news director can schedule special features, interviews, news in depth approaches. When there's a feature on Sunday afternoon on pros and cons of fluoridation, the salaries of local teachers, the local war on poverty, you'll be amazed how many will switch from TV baseball. If you have a policy of absolute maximum of five minutes for any type of talk show, including news, I'd reconsider. Local issues, which your community will discuss for weeks, can't be boiled down to three minutes.

I feel too many newsmen adopt the shock treatment. Rather than dig for worthwhile, meaningful news, they overemphasize the "thrill" element of minor local stories, and are always waiting for that "big break." Is there an over-playing of storm warnings? One reason the FCC is so stringent on emergency operations for daytime stations is due to some staying on the air after normal sign-off in order to advise of hurricanes hundreds of miles away. On the other hand, if one has a critical situation, the manager should keep the operation on the air. Just a year ago our daytimer in Muscatine was on a 24-hour operation for 18 days, during the Mississippi flood, with temporary studios set up in Emergency Manpower headquarters.

In order to keep our phone-in programs from becoming a complaint center, we plan a 20-minute section following the noon news, and find that more informative discussions result. We question the use, especially in small markets, of the syndicated phone-in show with its wide array of questionable and suggestive topics. In my book, a commercial for Diana's Dress Shop on West Second Street just does not fit into a half hour discussion on prostitution.

Don't mistake news for promotion and vice versa—a news department can be used for commercial promotion, but within limits. Don't let the sales manager become news director every time he has a new program account or promotion. Ed Shepherd, news director of the Iowa Radio Network, puts it this way: "Few things are more ludicrous than a newsman going into verbal ecstasies over the interior decor of a new supermarket."

More than ever before people are traveling to foreign countries. Are we taking full advantage of this interest? We're now programming a series of five-minute interviews I recorded last year in the Far East, as a section of an expanded newscast. For example, one afternoon in Macau I had the opportunity to speak through an interpreter with some 18 refugees just escaped from Red China. Although having been on the water for over nine hours, eluding Communist gun boats, they were still cooperative. The series has been used on the Iowa Radio Network, and is also being broadcast by other stations throughout the country.

For the past seven years we've produced two half-hour newscasts weekly for 2,500-3,000 Spanish-speaking migrant workers. Through an arrangement with area newspapers along the Texas border, we bring these families news from their home towns. The "Spanish News" is completely sold out.

How many local daily newspapers are delivered by mail a day late? Perhaps more than you realize. In many markets the Saturday edition goes to press in late morning. A death or accident occurring Saturday morning is not reported in the newspaper until Monday, which is not received in hundreds of homes until Tuesday —a lapse of over three days in print communications. Farm listeners have told us that if it were not for radio, a nearby farmer could die and be buried before they ever heard about it. A discussion with your postmaster may give you some worthwhile information.

Are newsmen setting up and keeping in touch with correspondents around the trade area? They can be invaluable—and news from surrounding communities certainly helps your area salesman. Make certain he is alerted to the value of news stories. For that matter, many stations do a great job in integrating every member of the staff as a news "stringer."

Some of our best human interest stories are being produced daily by one of of our advertisers. A large Indiana grain company recently purchased a local operation. The management not only wished a broadcast of grain prices but also to add a feature which would gain quick and enthusiastic response from farm families. We suggested they supply their salesmen with tape recorders and interview area people about farm operations, plus personal interest features. Mike Lawrence, who did the interviewing, never had a microphone in his hand before, but he has news sense. The five-minute feature is doing well, and the sponsor, Central Soya, is well pleased.

When the FFA group takes a farm tour—as they have done to the South and into Canada—we arrange to have the young men phone back a report on the day's activities. The sponsors receive only name credit on the program—commercials are given at other times of the day. In this way, you do not limit the number of advertisers. We follow this plan also on sports features.

What should local policy on news release be? Does the Chamber of Commerce secretary tell a newsman that "last night the Board of Directors took issue with the Rock Island Railroad on a rail crossing dispute, but we can't release the news until noon today—we want to be fair to the newspaper." Here is where a station manager must go to bat and get into the fray. Your news director needs your backing on this one. I've known stations to accept a news release at 2 or 3 P.M.! When radio gives up its speed and flexibility, it has 2½ strikes against it. You're selling your heritage. To ask radio to hold up its speed is the same as asking the newspaper to give up its pictures. You are there to serve your listeners. When you hold up news, it's a disservice to them and to your sponsors. If you can't get the Chamber of Commerce, United Fund or Fire Department to see it your way, tell your listeners about the situation. You'll get results, and if handled correctly, your prestige will go up a few points, too. With stations doing more editorializing I feel that news release problems, and other difficulties in this area, will tend to diminish.

In reference to our print brethren, we find it helps to set the record straight now and then. When newspaper stories carried articles on over-commercialization in broadcast media we did some stories in depth on ad content in print media, telling how second class mail privileges allow newspapers to average over 80% advertising content. In practice you'll find newspapers average about 65% of the space devoted to advertising, better than double the amount a radio Code subscriber will allow.

Another source of interest to listeners: many print media

wax emotional on freedom of the air waves, complain about broadcast programming and stress how the broadcast channels belong to the public. But these same editors are strangely silent on the subject of subsidies, through second class mailing privileges, to newspapers and magazines. Federal taxes must absorb 60-65% of the losses incurred in mailing the printed word, while air mail and first class have more than paid their way for many years. I've often thought that if the Post Office Department was an exacting in its numerous regulations of print media as the FCC is with broadcasters the world would have a different hue.

Broadcasters throughout the country have one great common concern, the critical shortage of trained people. The Journalism faculty at the University of Iowa recommended only one June graduate for a radio news opening. This young man, with no commercial experience, is going to a 5,000 watt network operation. In an effort to build newspaper interest among teachers and students the ANPA, eight years ago, instituted a Newspaper in the Classroom workshop. Over 900 teachers have attended. Broadcasters need to do more in this area.

We have our challenges and our problems. But certainly we can point, too, to the many fine accomplishments in local radio news operations. And these accomplishments will grow even larger as long as we remember never to underestimate the power and potential of radio news.

PART THREE

Modern Music

11. JOHN R. BARRETT
    Station Manager KRLA, Pasadena, California

12. PERRY B. BASCOM
    General Manager WBZ Radio, Boston, Massachusetts

13. DANNY WILLIAMS
    Program Manager WKY, Oklahoma City, Oklahoma

Several years ago, about the time rock and roll singer Elvis Presley left for the Army, I heard one of our broadcast brethren say: "This marks the beginning of the end of the big beat and maybe a new beginning for the big band." This well meaning broadcaster was dreaming, of course, for types like Take The A Train *and* Tuxedo Junction *have never returned again as top singles or albums.*

This doesn't mean to say that some of our most listened-to stations all over the country don't play big bands. They do. And there's no denying that a strong—and often vociferous—segment of the listening audience still prefers the big band sound. It has been the twang and heavy beat, though, that month after month, has commanded the attention of the young pace setters, the so-called in-crowd who set the music style pace for the country—indeed the whole world.

But what, we're always asked, is modern music? How does it differ from rock and roll or top 40 or contemporary? The fact is, it doesn't. And it's dangerous to try to give "it" a name or really try to define it. But this sound, which has taken over much of our airwaves—together with the goofy hair, tight pants, mod hats and unintelligible words—shows no signs of letting up, really. A dissection of the audience any time of the day reveals, clearly, that it's not only teens and sub-teens who feel the big beat, that frequent the discotheques, but the young housewives and even Mom and Dad.

"The Mommas and the Poppas," "The Rolling Stones," and the conservative but "in" Petula Clark have, more than any other factor, shaped the styles and the dances in addition to pop music.

This section might more aptly be called "Is The Big Beat Here To Stay?" For it is the big beat we're really addressing ourselves to. And intermingled with rock and roll or this big beat emerges the Nashville sound, which is a sort of combination of country music, rhythm and blues and the Liverpool sound.

11

JOHN R. BARRETT

John R. Barrett is the manager of KRLA, Pasadena, California. A native of Omaha, Nebraska, he graduated from the University of Nebraska with a degree in radio. He has been a disc jockey and program director at WTIX, New Orleans; news director at WHB, Kansas City; and, most recently, station manager of WKBW, Buffalo, New York. Mr. Barrett has also participated in a radio audience program at Tulane University.

MODERN RADIO, if I may begin on the abstract, is a specialized mood service. What we normally consider "modern radio," that is top 40 or pop music radio, is at the opposite end of the mood spectrum from the smooth music or violin station. A majority of listeners use one to reinforce a happy, carefree, big beat mood. They use the other to reinforce a relaxed mood. Obviously, the fewer responsibilities a person has, the more carefree he or she is. The normal freedom from the responsibility of adulthood, plus the population explosion, has given top 40 a vast audience among the young people. It doesn't follow that all top 40 listeners are teenagers, however. A search of today's society would probably reveal quite a few happy adults.

As for modern radio's lasting quality, if we are considering the abstract—that is, a specialized sound—I see top 40, or a mood service, as only scratching the surface. Specialized service can take many forms. I suggest that some of our daytime operators might take a cue from the highly successful women's magazines and try a specialized "housewife" station. Even with limited hours of operation in the winter, the station is on the air when the housewife is available. With the audience enjoying more and more leisure time, I can visualize an all-sports format—specializing in play-by-play, hunting, fishing, recreation and sports news. A glance at the magazine stands is all that is required to take home a dozen specializations applicable to modern radio.

Now, let us look at the surface scratcher—the top 40 station of 1966/67. If indeed, it is here to stay, what are *we* doing to contribute to its lasting power?

There are some interesting experiments being conducted in Los Angeles. One of the more basic, and controversial, of these experiments is the "limited commercial" policy. It is generally conceded that young listeners have a low tolerance for talk in any form, but these same young listeners are very important to modern radio because of the influence they exert on the family. Indeed, Dr. Paul Lazarsfeld, one of media's most respected researchers, tells us that the listener's choice of media is influenced primarily by the opinion of the female teenager.

Limiting commercials has several beneficial effects: more audience, a positive representation to the advertiser and a necessity for the station—setting the pace for the market—to enforce its rate card. The Los Angeles market's two primary top 40 contenders, KRLA and KHJ, both limit their commercial content to 10 minutes per hour. I am sure that Ken De Vaney of KHJ has been asked as often as I: "In the station's best interests, how can you afford to do this?" My answer is: "In the station's best interest, we can't afford *not* to do it."

In 1965 I made a statement that the FCC's requirements regarding surveying your community can be beneficial to you, as well as to the community. These community surveys do not have to end with service programming. They are especially valuable when applied to entertainment.

For instance, talking with listeners we found an increasing demand in Los Angeles for "oldies." Checking this against record sales, we found that certain oldies were outselling the top currently popular songs. This, obviously, revealed an area of entertainment not provided by our competition. The question then arose: how do you make the listener sit up and take notice of the fact that KRLA is offering them something a little bit different? Several years ago, in a smaller market, I engineered a campaign to call everybody in that city and tell them to listen to our station. In a city of a quarter of a million families, this was feasible. In Los Angles, with seven million people in the metropolitan area, this is impossible. The idea then was advanced that if we can't call them, why not let them call us?

The next question was obvious. Will they call and what does it take to motivate them to call? For the answer, we continued our community inquiry. This time, to the sociology department of the University of Southern California. We were lucky. Motivation is no problem. In a major urban area, life has become so depersonalized that people will use almost any excuse to talk with another human being. We found that excuse in record requests.

Toll-free lines from all parts of metropolitan Los Angeles were installed. The calls come in a separate office, where a staff of seven operators—most of them radio-television students from nearby colleges—answer the phones and take the requests. Hourly, the requests are tabulated for such information as the favorite oldies, the hour's most requested song, etc. Daily, the sheets are tallied into the next day's play list. Weekly, these play lists are tallied against the market's sales list. This enables us to check any obvious discrepancies.

Has this led to any change of format? No. The songs requested follow the sales lists very closely. What ratio of oldies to new songs are we playing? Presently, two new to one old, although the request demand has at times upped that ratio as high as one to one. Do the jocks exercise any control over the music? No. It is all pre-programmed according to formula, the same as a regular list.

Do you refuse requests? No. The only songs played—old or new—are those that are, or have been, on the top 40 lists at some time, and our operators have such lists on hand. The farther back we go, the more defined the list becomes until, let's say as of seven years ago, the list may be down to the top 40 songs of that year, not on a week-to-week basis. The phone operator checks the request against the list, and if the request doesn't appear, we have a brief pitch mimeo'd for their use that says: "I'm sorry, but that particular song is not in KRLA's library. Do you have a second choice?" So far, we have only used this reply twice in one month. The listener is never left with the impression that a request is going to be played, if it isn't. He's always asked for his second choice if we can't play the first. Listeners are as much influenced by the music they hear on the station as we are by their requests, and it's unlikely that a request would be made for music greatly out of context with our top 40 format.

Programming, therefore, *is* an area where a survey, or knowledge, of community tastes, can be of great benefit to a station.

In connection with programming, let us consider another area: the role of the personality in the modern format. If we continue from the premise that the listener's choice of radio fare is determined by his mood, we then can surmise that he chooses a modern format station because he wants to reinforce his upbeat, effervescent mood.

Many programmers mistakenly believe that, because a listener is looking for a modern, happy sound, the dj must be a laughing, perennially-happy, joke-telling type. I have never looked upon the dj as an entertainer, but rather as a coordinator. It is his job to blend all the elements of programming—music, commercials, public service announcements—into a listenable presentation. If the responsibility for the production of humorous material is put in the hands of the programming department, the station can be assured of a consistent quality—not always the case with the dj, whose performance varies as it does for all human beings. He's subject to moods, marital or extra-marital problems, receding hairlines, expanding waistlines, all matters of his concern.

The next logical question is: how does the programming department inject humor into your programming? Simple. You produce it. You create short, humorous spots.

Or, you can plan a funny giveaway. The Batman craze started about a year ago. We immediately came out with a "KRLA Bat Kit." We didn't play up the Bat Kit. In fact, we played it down. The Bat Kits were so popular, we were flooded with orders. In one month, we had shipped 60,000 Bat Kits. We stopped promoting the Kit, but the orders kept coming in. The most popular item in the Kit was a sheet of "sticky-type Bat dealies." These were stamps which could be pasted on school book covers, exam papers, doors—anywhere. They carried little messages such as "Robin eats worms" and "Batman for Governor." We then printed a second run of 50,000 new improved sticky-type Bat dealies, for a promotion we called "Son of Bat Dealie."

If you can't think of a funny promotion, you might try poking gentle fun at some of your community's idiosyncrasies or frustrations.

The light touch—humor—can be used in all types of station promotion. Even call letters can be turned to advantage. At KRLA, for instance, we have the KRL "A," a model "A" mobile unit—not the fastest or highest-flying in Los Angeles, perhaps, but pretty distinctive. And, the KRL Apes, our dj's basketball team that gives exhibition games at local schools.

How do we schedule these humor spots? We usually cut six per week, and use one per hour—24 hours per day. After much experimenting, this seems to carry the most impact. Fewer gives too frequent air exposure. More is a waste, since the average listener doesn't hear all six.

At the 1965 NAB clinics, the question of news in a top 40 format became an item of interest. Can you keep the kids for a newscast? Some said there was no hope. I disagreed. Today, more than ever before, kids *are* news. They make it, they're involved in it, they're concerned—whether it's draft protestors, the Vietnam Day Committee, or civil rights.

During the past year, our news department has done some interesting things in reporting, always with two aims in mind:

1. At all times make the material at hand interesting to young people. (This necessitates a lot of digging and a lot of rewrite.) If you can't make the material interesting to young people, find stories that are of interest to them. And if neither of those two work, take a page from the Hearst book: "You supply the pictures. I'll supply the War." And make news that's interesting.

2. Select interesting material. And here we're in an area where a station can perform a real service—and cannot only *keep* young listeners, but add them. Each week we select a topic of general interest for in-depth reporting. We research the topic and prepare a complete in-depth study, which is then broken into 30- or 45-second capsules.

In addition to the study of the draft, KRLA has done similar studies of narcotics, specifically marijuana and LSD. Student opportunities for summer employment, the phenomenon of UFO sightings, the Delano grape workers strike, protest songs, the role of Synanon, and the 1966 Alabama Democratic gubernatorial primary have all made interesting topics. At the end of a study of summer job availabilities for young people, we offered our listeners a guide outlining opportunities available to them, how to look for a job, where to look, etc.

In addition to serving as promos for the station, these weeklong capsulized studies can be of sufficient quality to win awards. Our analysis of the Watts riot, and what precipitated it, won us the California State Associated Press Award for Merit as the best, locally produced documentary.

Programming must, therefore, be regarded as a whole, not something composed of parts. The music and the dj may be the key to a successful, modern format but still only a portion. Programming is music and the djs, but it's well-integrated news too . . . and station promotion . . . and humor . . . all well-thought out and carefully-produced.

Modern radio is here to stay for as long as it remains modern. Espousal of the mass taste is often, by its very nature, unpopular, but a popular medium reflects popular, personal tastes. Radio must be as flexible as the changing needs and tastes of the public, if it is to truly *serve* the public.

By the intelligent use of surveys, analysis and tests, we can keep radio the flexible, portable, personal medium it is—keep it vital and contemporary, in a word, modern.

12

PERRY B. BASCOM

Perry B. Bascom, general manager of WBZ, Boston, Massachusetts, joined the Group W stations (Westinghouse Broadcasting Co.) in 1956. He served as eastern sales manager for radio and TV, national radio sales manager, and general manager of KYW, Cleveland, Ohio, before assuming his present position in 1965. Born in Bound Brook, New Jersey, Mr. Bascom attended Bowdoin College and served in the Naval Air Corps during World War II.

WE AT WBZ believe that the majority of the American public will always want new and different music, music which reflects the time in which it lives. Going one step further, I urge you to *not* play this kind of music—unless, of course, you are prepared to accept the awesome liability that playing modern music brings. You'll find yourself swamped with audience response: letters, phone calls, tours, requests for personal appearances, calls to trace lost dogs, to come to the aid of a local charity, to help a college freshman write a term paper on radio and on-and-on. It's a fact of broadcasting life that when you play popular music—that music which most appeals to the broadest cross-section of the American public—you'll find yourself *intimately* involved with your audience.

I'm not trying to create the impression that our audience is a lot of trouble. On the contrary, we're happy that such a large audience relies on us. We welcome it. And we're also happy about the kind of audience that this modern music attracts.

Eighty percent of our adult male audience and 83% of our adult female audience are between 18 and 50. In fact, our total adult audience, 18 and over, is about 80%. We have more housewives between 6:00 A.M. and 6:00 P.M than any other two stations *combined*. More professional and technical, managerial and executive male listeners, 6 to 6, than any other station—and more families with three or more members than the next two stations combined during those same time periods.

Income? Right down the middle, with about half our audiences family income between $5,000 and $10,000. And that's the kind of audience profile that keeps the advertiser happy too.

The public will always be interested in modern music, but just what is modern music?

We had long suspected that people use the phrase, "rock and roll," in describing music they do not like, while they might call music they prefer by a more palatable name such as "jazz," "swing," or even "modern music." So we ran a survey in one of the Group W markets and found that, of all those people who listen to modern music, only 37% called it rock and roll. It's interesting how people listen and how they describe their listening.

But let's look at rock and roll, swing, or whatever you want to call it and see where it came from. The history of American music in many ways parallels American military and economic history. After each of our three major World Wars in the past 100 years, there has been a tremendous popularity of basically emotional or non-technical music. Following the Civil War it was "ragtime." After World War I it was called "Dixieland" and contained the same derivations. Then after World War II a musically sophisticated America found a new exciting emotional brand of music in the South and called it, among many names, "rock and roll."

Now, just as it was with ragtime and Dixieland, here was a brand of music that was elementary in its composition, requiring little formal knowledge. It could be played by soloists or small groups; it was very danceable. So the American public bought it and are still buying it by the millions of records today. There is no doubt about it, the musical form commonly called rock and roll is now a very much recognized and established part of our American musical heritage.

There is a very strong trend toward the inter-marriage of the three classifications of ragtime, Dixieland and rock and roll. Within the last five years we've witnessed a strong interaction between rock and roll and country and western music. At the same time, we're hearing more and more of the basic rhythms of rock and roll in our jazz music. There's also a new sound to rhythm and blues—basically informal music with a formal symphonic background.

America now has a many faceted popular music, not just three basic classifications. As more mutations of music are developed with this interchange of emotional and formal music, we'll have even newer and more interesting popular musics that will reflect the time and the tempo of our lives. We as broadcasters don't set the musical pace. Our audiences do this for us. What we decide to play simply mirrors the tastes of the particular segment of the public we decide to serve. Yes, a given station actually has the ability to pick and choose its audience. And, just as the so-called soft music stations can identify with various portions of an audience interested in soft music, so it is with the modern popular music stations.

What has modern music done for WBZ? For a limited number of years, prior to 1960, following our declaring independency from a radio network, WBZ Radio maintained a share of audience in the Boston market that was certainly substantial. But the station was not the most popular station. Since 1961, when our musical product assumed a more contemporary, modern or popular sound, there has been continued audience growth. Now we enjoy a fine margin of advantage over our nearest competitor.

I have used the term "musical product" above. Quite obviously there is much more to WBZ and to most stations in the United States than just the music. WBZ Radio personalities are strong, readily-identifiable, community-involved individuals; the music is in a contemporary vein, with broad mass appeal; and the news and public affairs activities can best be described as tireless, aggressive, and alert to the needs and interests of the community. It is the policy of WBZ Radio to develop the entertainment responsibilities and potential of the facility as fully as possible. WBZ presents public affairs, public service, editorials and news programs in a showmanlike manner.

In the opening of this article, I said that we have an "awesome liability to the public." With such popularity as we enjoy, one must be constantly alert to the needs of the community and speak forthrightly to these needs. One method of doing this is concerned with the right, and obligation, that we all have as broadcasters: to editorialize. I urge you to use this right, if you are not doing so. In 1965, WBZ broadcast 234 editorials covering some 61 different editorial subjects. We broadcast 29 newscasts daily, including one 30-minute newscast, four 10-minute newscasts and the others 5-minutes in length. This keeps our listeners informed and involved in newsworthy events. We buttress the news and editorial activity with news specials and documentaries on timely, significant and controversial subjects. We devote 90 minutes, Monday through Friday, to the "Bob Kennedy/*Contact*" Show, following our half-hour news—with Bob and his guests being able to carry on a spirited dialogue with the public by means of telephone procedure, where you as the listener hear both ends of the conversation.

Our premise is to involve our listeners. As such, the promotions we do, both on-the-air and off-the-air, represent a significant contribution to many worthwhile organizations when we are able to muster the interests and the activities—and sometimes the pocketbook—of our listeners on behalf of worthwhile causes. Our contests are interesting, exciting and unusual ways for our public to participate with us.

Although my basic assignment here was on the subject of modern or popular music, I felt it necessary to roam and touch on some of the other ingredients of a most successful broadcast operation. Actually, WBZ represents a composite of most of the stations represented in this book.

Popular music *is* here to stay—not really because of the mass media exposure but due to the fact that people like it, want it and create the demand for it, just as they have been doing during the countless centuries of musical history.

Who knows what will be the next advance in the evolution of popular music? But WBZ will be playing it. And, as a broadcaster and a man who enjoys this vibrant and unpredictable reflection of American history, I can only hope that I have sense enough to recognize it when it happens. Yes, quite possibly, a new brand of popular music is just around the corner. I'm delightedly anxious to hear it and participate in its presentation.

13

DANNY WILLIAMS

For 17 years Mr. Williams was a staff announcer for WKY Radio in Oklahoma City, Oklahoma and was known to a wide listening audience as an early morning man on "Time And Tune Parade." He serves also in a dual capacity as program director on WKY Radio. In addition to this dual capacity, he hosts his own mid-day variety show, "Danny's Day," on WKY TV, Monday through Friday.

EVERYONE in broadcasting has heard what almost has become a cliché in our business: "We're in communications and we can't even communicate with one another!" A part of this derives from the fact that so many of the terms used in our business are meaningless. We use words which *connote* a great deal, but *denote* very little. In the field of music there are more meaningless, totally subjective terms used than in any other facet of broadcasting.

Let us try to define all of the terms—that is, to define them *relative* to the way we use them. Though perhaps we should define "modern" first, it is—in the context of this essay—an adjective which modifies the noun "music." This word alone elicits many different definitions. The dictionary gives very little help as it refers to music as a science, to wit: "The science or art of pleasing, expressive, or intelligible combination of tones; the art of making such combinations, especially into compositions of definite structure and significance."

Frankly this definition is poor, because a great many noises labeled music, which you hear as individuals, are *not* pleasing to you, express *very little,* and exhibit little if any intelligence. You will probably also agree that many of these tones labeled music have very little structure and certainly no significance; herein is where Webster and anybody who tries to define music academically fall far short. Because music must be heard by somebody, and that somebody is perhaps pleased or displeased—or, perhaps, affected somewhere in between—and the amount of expressiveness, intelligibility or, for that matter, the appreciation of the structure or significance of the music is completely dependent on each individual.

Thus, music becomes a subjective experience. Or, to put it more precisely and clearly, with most of us music is an *emotional* experience. To be sure, there are musicians who have an academic interest in music, but at the moment we are not interested in the four movements of the symphony or, for that matter, the mathematical progression inherent in the vibrations of a drum head.

For this reason, our definition of music will have to include the person hearing the noises and tones and rhythms called music. And, since that person's response is largely emotional, we will say that music is noises and tones, arranged rhythmically, which stimulate an emotional response from an individual hearing it. You will note that we have not used nebulous terms like "good" or "bad," because these reactions are dependent as much on the person responding as on the music stimulating. We have not used equally nebulous terms such as "rock and roll," "country and western," "big band," or "popular," nor have we as yet used "modern," because, it, too, is a word often vague in connotation.

We believe that all of these labels—rock and roll, country and western, et cetera, and good and bad—in terms of our definition of music—have to do with *response,* and I would further add that these terms and labels cannot be defined except in terms which are completely subjective and, therefore, may have as many definitions as there are personalities.

We can do a little better with "modern" and "popular" if we apply them to *groups* of people rather than to individuals. Modern used to be practically synonymous with "new," but in our opinion it has come to mean "what's in fashion" and, therefore, modern has something to do with *time*. At one time, high-button shoes were modern—they were in fashion at a particular time. Paul Whiteman music was, at a particular time, modern—and, for that matter, Gregorian chants. So we must place modern in the dimension of time. Modern things, consequently, have been with us in the past, are with us in the present and will be with us in the future. We might, then, define modern as that which is "in fashion" with a particular group at a particular time. We would further add that popular is practically synonymous with modern.

At this point, it may appear to some that this is a composition on semantics rather than modern music and its relation to broadcasting—or programming in radio, which is the whole point. But without these definitions and explanations of what we mean by modern music, we can never hope to present something of value to anyone connected with radio programming.

By definition, what is modern in music today is as dependent on the audience as the music itself and, consequently, there are many types of music played on radio today which, to a particular group, are modern. We dare say that the manager of any radio station offering music today feels that the music his station plays is in fashion with a *certain group of people* and, therefore, is modern music by definition.

The size of that group, to be sure, is a very important consideration to us as broadcasters. Each of us would like to have the largest audience, and if we can't have the largest group, the next largest and so on. There is, so far as we have been able to determine, no single type of music being presented on record or live today that appeals to everybody. Musical taste is not, like "air-breathing," a homo sapiens trait but, rather, acquired and, though it may be the only common denominator for a particular group of people, these people may differ substantially as individuals.

For instance, all people who buy Buck Owens records don't live on the farm, nor are they all 18, nor do they all drop out of school at 14. All the people who like Beatle records do not have long hair, are not under 21 and are not in the lower 5% in propensity to consume. All the people who listen to and appreciate music by Leonard Bernstein do not have PhDs, are not Jewish and do not spend $20,000 per year on consumer products.

In determining what sort of music to play to your particular group, the primary prerequisite is objectivity. We would postulate that a great deal of the success achieved by some so-called top 40 radio stations was due to the fact that station management introduced objectivity into the selection of music by using empirical data in concluding what to play and not to play. Too much music played on the radio in the past, currently and, we're afraid, in the future, is "in fashion" with a group of *one*. He may be the manager, the program director or he may be the disc jockey on the air. His responses are the only factor determining what is modern or not modern or,—even more dangerous so far as gaining or losing audience is concerned—determining what's "good" or "bad."

There are many groups today insofar as music is concerned; the labels abound—top 40, rock and roll, pop, modern, country and western, religious, good—and since music is in essence an emotional experience, there will probably always be varied tastes. Exactly how music will sound or how people will react only time will tell. Whether the music a broadcaster is playing currently (or, to put it another way, whether that music which is modern with your audience at this time in history) will be with us tomorrow, only the development of people's tastes can tell.

Hence, we come to the main point which we are to clarify: "Modern Music, Here To Stay." In the declarative sense of the statement we would say *yes!* This "yes" is predicated on observations of the past. Since time began—or, to be more explicit, since history has been recorded—man has reacted to music, and a particular type of music has been "in fashion" with particular groups. To be sure, it has not always sounded the same, had the same instrumentation, rhythm or subject matter but, through the ages, all peoples and cultures have reacted to some form of music. Since this has been true and seems to be inherent in the nature of man, we believe it is safe to assume that this will be true in the future.

Posed as a *question:* "Is Modern Music Here To Stay?" the answer would be *no*. Future generations will react differently from those of today; the world will be different; it will probably move at a different pace and values will be different from the values of similar music groups today. Almost everyone connected with the broadcast business plays some kind of music—and, since we have more or less said that all of that music is modern, I imagine each of us has wondered if the music we are currently playing will still be played next year or ten years from now. Some of it probably will be, because we will make that great broadcast mistake of deciding we are average and what *we* like, *everyone* likes—or, that our friends, who are pretty much like us, represent an adequate sample and, if they like the music we play, everyone else does. However, when Hooper or Pulse comes up with a rating based on 700 to 1,000 people sampled at random, we'll scream and yell and say the sample is too small, that it cannot be projected to the total audience? While still shouting and berating the ratings, we'll form a committee of one and project our tastes in music on our entire audience and then wonder why Hooper is wrong and Pulse is wrong and so very few people are listening.

Since we have no idea what the modern music many stations are playing sounds like, what its label is, or what group it appeals to, we could not begin to prognosticate its longevity. We do believe that determining music for people is a continuing and sometimes difficult process. We believe that tastes in music have always been changing and will continue to change. These changes are not always broad; many of them are subtle; many of these changes catch on quickly; some seem to grow on groups of people.

If we hope to be successful and keep our music as "modern" as possible, we must be as close to our audience as possible . . . we must be aware of their tastes in music and try to reflect these tastes.

PART FOUR

Country Music

14. DAN MCKINNON
    President, KSON, San Diego, Calif.

15. GEORGE G. DUBINETZ
    Vice president and General Manager, WJJD, Chicago, Ill.

16. R. E. THOMLINSON
    General Manager, KTAR, Eugene, Oregon

17. DALE PETERSON
    General Manager, KGBS Radio, Los Angeles, Calif.

18. JERRY GLASER
    Director, Country Music Association

Regardless of where one looks or listens, country music has become an increasingly integral part of modern radio programming. In fact, today's country sound has found more popularity in big cities than in "hillbilly" country and seems to be increasing in popularity almost as fast among professional people as it is among so-called blue collar workers.

There are many elements in country music today that appeal to a wide variety of different types of people. The music is tuneful and has a beat. The lyrics are simple and direct, and they tell a happy, a melancholy or moral story in song.

Whether you call it the "Nashville sound," "modern country and western sound," "the countrywide sound," or "countrypolitan," more of America's radio stations each month are programming this truly American music with great audience-building success. And more of a wide variety of listeners are finding pleasure in this type of music.

14

DAN McKINNON

Dan McKinnon is a native Californian, born in San Bernardino January 27, 1934. He served as a page boy in Congress from 1950 through 1952. Graduating from the University of Missouri in 1956, he received his commission in the United States Navy shortly after graduation. Since February, 1962, Mr. McKinnon has served as president and general manager of KSON-AM and KSEA-FM, College Grove Center, San Diego, Calif.

MANY PEOPLE think country music sounds the same today as it did years ago when it was commonly referred to as "hillbilly music." The latter, combined with the disc jockey who constantly talked down to his listeners, caused many to turn their noses in the air and walk away from country music. This is where country music stood until the middle 50's when the *modern* country sound started to be listened to more and more each day.

People from all walks of life—with both low and high incomes—started to listen to and appreciate the fresh new *modern* country sound. Modern country music still offers the nostalgia—the touch of back home—and yet, it is still down-to-earth music with which anyone can relate himself or someone he knows.

Most country music songs are written about everyday experiences of people. Today, just as in the past, people are interested primarily in other people and their experiences. Country music is kept relatively simple and, as a result, requires very little concentration to listen to and understand. In a world made up of so many busy people, it's easy to see why many of them favor country music.

A country music station that programs the modern country sound doesn't assume its listeners to be people who can be, or should be, talked down to. The disc jockey speaks sincerely to the loyal country music fans but in a fresh modern and friendly manner. When we refer to our listeners as being loyal, we mean that these people respond more readily to us when we suggest a particular sponsor with whom they should do business.

The audiences are also loyal to the extent they generally stay tuned to the country music station throughout each day. They listen by choice and, therefore, they are usually more easily sold on what you have to say than a person who might have tuned in by chance.

As a modern country music station, we know a person doesn't need to be a swinger to enjoy a Sinatra or Ella. It's not necessary to be an intellectual to enjoy a symphony, nor an illiterate clod-buster to appreciate the smooth style of one of country music's favorites—the great Jim Reeves.

This is just one sample of the music we refer to as modern country music which has been with us since the mid-50's. This is regarded as the period when country music really progressed into the popular form of music that it is today. During the 50's, such hits as these became million sellers: *Your Cheatin' Heart, Don't Let The Stars Get In Your Eyes, Sixteen Tons, Satisfied Mind, The Battle of New Orleans.*

The basic ingredients that have made country music so successful are the toe tapping rhythms and lyrics with empathy. The country music artists and bands now reflect the modern musical culture, heritage and tradition of their times—just as the early old country fiddlers and instrumentalists of 40 years ago reflected the mode of their times. The sound of country music comes from the instruments.

In a country music band, there are generally guitars, drums, steel guitars, base and often a piano. Other instruments that are sometimes used are the dobro guitar, which resembles a flat top guitar but is played in about the same manner as a steel guitar, the fiddle, commonly referred to as a violin by symphony orchestras and banjos, both five string and tenor. It is rare, however, that a wind instrument is mixed with country music.

The five string banjo is always used to make up bluegrass music, sometimes referred to as hoedown or hillbilly music. We don't play a great deal of this type of music, although it has become better known as folk music and has developed such well known stars as Bill Monroe, referred to as the founder of bluegrass music and, perhaps the best known bluegrass group of them all, Flatt & Scruggs. These artists and others like them make hundreds of personal appearances at various colleges throughout the country each year and individually have sold millions of records.

This type of folk music is not just protest music, but grassroots heritage. Our listeners realize we're not calling this a gorgeous piece of music but an authentic bit of Americana that goes back to all our ancestors. It's easy to understand, at this point, why country music is still referred to today as the music from America's heart.

In the past 10 years, part of the new sound that country music has added is the voice of the female vocalist. These include such all-time greats as Patsy Cline, Kitty Wells and such pop artists as Kay Starr, Jo Stafford and Patti Page, who all sang with western swing bands at one time.

What makes the country music listener so loyal? Why does the missile engineer in San Diego remain loyal to the music he listened to as a youngster (or maybe his parents listened to country music). There are many reasons, the foremost of which, we feel, is the subject matter of the majority of country and western music. It's all entertainment—no snob appeal attempted. If the listener can't relate to any given song, the chances are he knows someone who can. Kitty Wells has been referred to as the "Queen of Country Music" for the last decade. There's a good reason why, too. It's the sincere delivery of songs which are part of everyday life.

There is humor, too. It isn't necessary for one to have lived a rural life to realize Billy Ed Wheeler was making memories when he wrote and recorded *Ode To The Little Brown Shack Out Back*.

As you may be aware, this type of music has blossomed record sales. *Life* Magazine did a recent story pointing out that 50 million country music records were sold last year. That is 40 percent of the total record sales!

15

GEORGE G. DUBINETZ

Mr. Dubinetz served as an account executive with the National Broadcasting Company from 1955 to 1958 at which time he joined the Robert E. Eastman Company as vice president and midwest manager. In December, 1964, he became general manager of WJJD, Chicago, a position he now holds.

I CAN'T SHARE any magical or mystical formulas for the success of country and western programming, simply because there aren't any. All you need are some c & w records and a friendly, down-to-earth dj and you've got it made. If there are any skeptics who think country music isn't red hot and spreading faster than a prairie grass fire, let me point out a few things that should remove all doubts from your minds.

The Country Music Association reports that stations are switching to c & w programming at the rate of one per day—and I'm sure these station owners made thorough investigations before they decided to switch.

How many of you remember the early 1966 issue of the *Saturday Evening Post?* Or the issue several months later of *Newsweek* that devoted its entire music section to c & w? You also might remember the subsequent articles on c & w in *Time* and *Life* magazines. And in our trade press: The *Broadcasting* Special Report titled, "Growing Sound of Country Music," and *Variety*'s story,

"Country AM's Go To Town." *Billboard* and *Cashbox* have had innumerable articles on the progress of c & w music and the success it is enjoying.

Locally, we've had things like the headline in the Sunday *Chicago Sun Times,* "Country Music Goes To Town." And another *Sun Times* article, "C & W Sweeps Grammys." And the headline of Chicago's *Sunday American,* "Nashville, Home of Country and Western."

Seldom does a week pass that some national magazine, trade publication, newspaper or TV network doesn't expound on the fabulous success of the "Nashville sound," or the "modern country & western sound," the "countrywide sound," "countrypolitan" —or whatever name some editor, columnist or programmer wants to give it for the moment.

Let's dissect country music and do an exploratory on just what it is that has caught the nation's musical fancy. The opening line of the *Newsweek* story is as follows, "The phenomenon called 'Nashville sound' yields about as easily to definition as relativity." It really isn't as complicated as some people try to make it appear. I don't think a definition is that important, for it's like trying to define what is a good painting. To someone it might be composition; to another, color; to another, subject or technique or mood. It's a lot of things that appeal to a lot of people.

The same thing is true with today's country & western sound —there are a lot of things about it that appeal to a lot of people. The music is tuneful and easy to remember, the lyrics are simple and direct and tell a happy, a melancholy or moral story in song. This music deals with people's emotions. You don't have to come from Tennessee to know what a broken heart is. It doesn't rely on gimmick sounds or a fad. The men are manly and the women feminine—and that alone is refreshing.

While country & western music has been around for many many years, I frankly don't think it could have grown as fast in popularity, say 10 years ago, as it has the past two or three years even with the same press and equal amount of exposure on radio and television. It has been in a process of evolution, and many things have contributed to its development. Any one single item being insignificant by itself, but each one like a piece of a jig-saw puzzle, important enough to help make it a complete picture. It probably started with World War II which brought people together from every section of the country. Northern GI's stationed in the south and southwest heard this music and took a liking to it.

The guitar, a basic instrument in c & w, found its place in rock music. As a matter of fact, the story goes that the Everly Brothers, on tour in England, showed the Beatles the instrumentation technique they use. The guitar has had the greatest revival of any instrument in the history of music.

As some country artists drifted to pop and folk and back again to country, there was a cross pollination of these sounds which resulted in identifiable similarities in many areas of our music. Then, as some stations began to program country and western and record sales began to increase, the artists, the arrangers and the composers began to come up with fresh material that further popularized the country and western sound.

And now, the range of country and western extends well beyond the specialized and limited audience that rock and roll, blues or folk music appeals to. Country and western has a broad audience base because the sound has appeal to the teenager as well as grandmother, the sophisticate as well as the plebian. I don't think there are many forms of music that can equal the broad appeal of country & western music in tempo, arrangements, instrumentation, beat and composition. For instance, here is a typical list of the full range of country music:

Rockabilly	*You're Right*/Don Winters
Western	*El Paso*/Marty Robbins
Blue Grass	*Salty Dog*/Osborne Bros.
Modern Country	*King of the Road*/Roger Miller
Pure Country	*See the Big Man Cry Mama*/Charlie Louvin
Folk Country	*Tupelo Country Jail*/Stonemans
Standard	*I Can't Stop Loving You*/Don Gibson
Continental Country	*Time Changes Everything*/Jimmy Dean
Recitation	*Men In My Little Girl's Life*/Archie Campbell
Religious Country	*These Things Shall Pass*/Johnny Cash
Classical Country	*Tennessee Waltz*/Arthur Fiedler

As you can see, the old weatherbeaten image that country music is a conglomeration of squeaky fiddles, twangy guitars, scratching washboards, musical saws and jug whistling is a thing of the past. The raw nasal "hillbilly" sound has been replaced by the smooth soft vocals like Eddie Arnold, Jimmy Dean, Bill Anderson, Jan Howard, Sonny James, all backed by choral groups that could easily qualify for any Broadway musical. The instrumentation includes the electric guitar, sweeping strings, trombones, electric organ, drums, an occasional French horn and even the harp. The music left the barn and moved to the concert hall—from the Eighth Street Theatre to McCormick Place, Carnegie Hall, the Houston Astro Dome, and the Miami Auditorium. The evening gown and the tux moved in beside the calico dress and checked shirt audience.

Let's zero in on what happens when a radio station owner takes the plunge and switches from a pop, rock, middle-of-the-road, or what-have-you format to country and western.

WJJD did just that—switched from a pop standard format to c & w in February 1965. When the official word was out that we were going to make the switch, *Billboard* came out with an editorial which I will quote in part: "We applaud the WJJD move. Country music represents an enormous and rich treasury of fine songs and fine artists, and this material properly programmed, could build a large, loyal body of listeners in the nation's No. 2 market. We hope, therefore, that a lot of thought will be given to every aspect of the station's programming. The country field contains true enchantment for the listener and record buyer, sales power for the advertiser and broadcaster. A smart programmer is the catalyst."

Let me assure you a lot of thought went into it. The switch was no snap decision, for before I joined the station, Harold Krelstein, President of Plough Broadcasting, had been having studies made of c & w record sales in the market, consultations with record companies and the Country Music Association, market and demographic analyses, and the necessary technical, equipment, and staff changes.

All the statistics seemed to indicate that the Midwest was ready for a major c & w station. A nation-wide record sales survey by the Record Industry Association of America disclosed that Illinois and the five adjacent states accounted for the highest share of all c & w album sales in the nation—23% of total sales, with little or no exposure of this music by radio stations in the area. The hard core of c & w music fans that we felt we would attract immediately were the "blue collar" workers, and 62.7% of Chicago's total population is comprised of blue collar workers. Because Chicago is highly industrialized, the market is highly unionized, so the average income of the tradesmen, craftsmen, machine operators is over $8700 annually as compared to the average income for the market of $7,748. Better than that, 25% are making over $10,000 annually.

The response was instantaneous—unsolicited letters by the thousands poured in daily. You may not believe it, but we read just about every one of the first 25,000 we received. While that mail was predominantly from blue collar families, it was interesting to see many letters from businessmen, executives, teachers, doctors, lawyers, college students. I even got a call from a minister complimenting WJJD on behalf of his congregation. The rating services felt this audience growth almost immediately, for in a few months, WJJD moved from dead last—we owed *Pulse* a few listeners—to fourth position in the market in three months.

This should be the time that the story ends with "they lived happily ever after." But it wasn't all peaches and cream, for we weren't carrying guitars full of money to the bank.

With the change in format, we knocked all the sponsored programs off the station and tripled our rate. We had very little national business before our change, because we didn't have any ratings, and the guy who was paying $15 a spot wasn't about to pay $50 a spot the next morning.

We had to go after new local advertisers and national accounts who were accustomed to paying top rate on other stations. Agencies listened politely to our story, and between yawns, buyers promised to give us a close look the next time around.

We had two things going against us. When we'd say c & w there were those who thought we had gone to the "Old Barn Dance" format that WLS had abandoned years ago, or that we were reviving the "Suppertime Frolics" and would be selling baby chicks and tombstones by mail order. Few buyers outside of Chicago had any idea of our audience profile or just didn't want to believe us. Country & western was fine out west or down south where there were cowboys and hillbillies and the music was native to the area—but not in Chicago!

We had a lot of proving to do, and we did it with live c & w shows where we invited agency people, the Country Music Association brought in a terrific show to Chicago that was hosted by the Sales Executives and Marketing Club where about 500 agency people attended as guests. The CMA again brought in a c & w show to the *Advertising Age* magazine's Summer Workshop, which is attended by ad managers and agency personnel from across the nation.

Resistance was beginning to weaken for our ratings continued to rise. Now, the buyers wanted qualitative data—just who are those nuts that like c & w music?

Here are a few of our current typical advertisers:

Budweiser	Schlitz	Pabst Brewing Co.
Old Milwaukee	Hamms Beer	Meister Brau
Dr. Pepper	Coca Cola	Pepsi Cola
Colgate-Palmolive	Anacin	Sylvania Electric
Seaboard Finance	C E T	Beneficial Finance
American Express	Kellogg's	Oscar Meyer
Quaker Oats	Swift & Co.	A & P
Korvette	United Biscuit	Sears
American Tobacco	Liggett & Meyers	R. J. Reynolds
P. Lorillard	Suzuki	Tobacco Co.

By the way, our rates went up in November 1965, and went up again in July 1966. Our billing has tripled, and we're doing it with 12 to 14 spots per hour.

Now, I can bring the story to a happy ending, but before I do, let me answer an inevitable question: What's the future of country & western music in broadcasting?

It couldn't be better! Country music is constantly being upgraded all the way from the recording studio to the delivery over the air. Everytime a pop artist has a hit with a country song or our music makes a pop chart, we gain new listeners. Everytime our music takes a Grammy award or our artists appear in concert or c & w is the subject of a TV spectacular, we gain more stature.

I read in *Billboard* that a great country catalog for the standard and educational field is underway. These are arrangements for concert band, stage band, choral groups, marching bands, concert orchestras, etc. The arrangers working on this are Richard Maltby, Richard Hayman, John Cacavas and others. Cacavas stated, "We are dressing up country music—putting it in a pop-educational context—because this is today's pop music."

Experts in the field of music all predict that pop and country & western will become one. One will absorb the other and I'll give you one guess who will be the dominant one. Country music has staying power. We're playing songs composed 25 years ago and they're still a hit. We have artists that are just as popular today as they were 25 years ago—this is why c & w will emerge as the new pop sound.

EXPLANATION OF SOME COUNTRY WESTERN STYLES

Rockability: A rock beat with twangy instruments. You can use a fiddle in rockabilly but a rock tune does not have fiddles.

Western: There is no back beat—instead it's more of a roll. Country has a basic beat but western has no solid beat in the background.

Blue Grass: Music without amplification of instruments; use strings —banjo dobro, mandolin with no rigging. Often includes three part harmony singing—lead alto and tenor with a twangy sound. Usually doesn't have more than 4 or 5 chord changes in the entire song.

Modern Country: Obvious absence of twang in voices. Instrumentation includes sweeping strings, piano, brass and choral groups in background.

Pure Country: Basic country band with lead guitar, bass, steel guitar, drums and fiddle. Often you will hear fiddle play in harmony with steel guitar.

Folk Country: Amplified lead guitar with predominantly string instruments. Much more complicated chording—have as many as 20 chords with minor and diminished chords.

Continental Country: Distinct foreign rythms with country instrumentation. Ethnic melodies that lend themselves to country arrangements, i.e., Irish ballads, German, Spanish, Mexican, etc. songs that usually are the native folk tunes.

16

R. E. "BOB" THOMLINSON

Mr. Thomlinson began his broadcast career at KJR, Seattle, Washington in 1927 as an engineer. From 1930 to 1951, he served as announcer, chief announcer and director of special events at KGW in Portland, Oregon. He was appointed general manager of radio stations KATR, Eugene; KAPT, Salem and KSHA, Medford—all Oregon—in June, 1963.

THIS IS THE story of Radio KATR, a nice little radio station in Eugene, Oregon that had a net loss after depreciation for the single month of November, 1963 of $4,800. Something had to be done and done quickly.

The general situation was this. There are eight AM stations and three FM's plus two VHF TV's and one healthy daily newspaper in the Eugene-Springfield market. Eugene is a city of 72,000 and Springfield, two miles away, has 22,000, and there are about 100,000 more in the trade area. Portland stations, 90 miles away, get some listeners but have no commercial impact locally.

Looking at the program competition of Eugene-Springfield, there were rock 'n' roll, middle-of-the-road, quasi religious, classical music, sports stations, and four full-time network affiliates in the crowded market—in addition two independent FM's.

The eight radio stations run 1,000 to 10,000 watts and are scattered from one end of the dial to the other. Five stations are crowded together in the area 1280 kcs to 1600 kcs. Radio KATR was only 18 months old on 1320 kcs and operated day time only with 1000 watts. I guess we could say that "prospects were not overly bright."

The November 1963 net loss of $4,800 called for drastic action. After study of what everybody in the market was doing—we elected to go country & western. On December 3, 1963 when nearly everybody was playing Christmas music we hit the air with all-day-long country and western. We stood out like a sore thumb, and the telephones rang merrily all day long. Action—motivation—country & western music had arrived in Eugene.

That's *why* and *how* we switched to country & western. None of the ideas expressed here are new. But the use of certain ideas grouped together seems to have hit a happy successful note for the finance department. Our station profits have shown consistent gains.

This is *how* we do it:

We are strictly music and news (we rip and read news of the AP news machine.) No local news men.

We cater to lumber industry people because Eugene is in the center of America's last great area of big trees. The hard working people of the timber spaces for reasons of their own prefer c & w music.

We cater to horse shows, western parades, the Hunt Club, and the annual local rodeo. Our area is loaded with horses. We encourage all our people to belong to at least one of the social, civic, fraternal clubs.

We occasionally sponsor at the local fairgrounds auditorium a western show featuring a nationally known singer and western band. Fee for this runs $1,200-$2,000, but we make money at it. We are not in western stage show business, but if we don't do the sponsoring some traveling promoter will bring in the show, and this leaves the country & western station with left over problems by association. We are damned if we do and damned if we don't—so we *do* the shows.

Our music runs the full play of western music. However, we do not use double-meaning lyric's or off-color stuff. By the way only a few *girls' records* are used. There are not very many good female artists in this field for some reason.

We prepare our own top-30 list each week from trade journals and local record shops and distribute locally to music shops. This list is also mailed promptly to record distributors in the Northwest and the national production shops. This pays off in plenty of free records. Our librarian has been working in c & w for eight years, and you need that experience in selecting music.

Musically, we use very little group singing except for the one per hour religious hymn which should run two minutes only. (You can sell each one of these.)

We play requests but never dedicate or announce that the song was requested.

After a commercial announcement, we go right into music without any comment. Should we double spot (and we do a lot of it) we separate the spots by a station ID, jingle, or a brief weather and time comment, or a short public service spot. We talk *into* but not *after* commercials.

We have only one 15-minute sponsored newscast at 7:15 A.M. The other newscasts at the half hour run five minutes only throughout the day to sunset.

Such talk programs as we present are limited to five minutes except for politicals. Political announcements are limited to 30 or 60 seconds—no 10-second name mentions are allowed.

Our announcers are all experienced men with a man's voice. We seek the 30-35 mature voice. Announcers are friendly but do not talk with tobacco juice on their face. They do not talk down to the audience about anything. Policywise we feature the music, *not* the announcer. Fees are not paid for any announcing job.

Promotionwise we do not use the newspaper and spend very little money on promotions except on the western shows—which generally make money. That, too, depends on the artist; we only sponsor the best.

We do sell a lot of remotes, where we play records, talk briefly to visitors, and give away 7-Up and odds and ends from the record library. We've done $9,000 in remotes in two years time at realty open houses, used car lots, grocery stores, department stores and grand openings.

Salesmen work four hours announcing on either Saturday or Sunday. This keeps them informed and current on what the station program policies are. This also takes care of the weekend part time problem.

The station has some unique ID's that we dreamed up for ourselves. These promote the station identification and at the same time salute one of the 45 small towns of our area. These jingles have brought us 350 letters and telephone calls asking "when is their town being saluted."

We are very careful not to talk about country music in anything but approving fashion. The people who regularly listen to country & western believe that *it* is the *good* music, and *so it is!* Radio KATR recently was offered a contract for a regional bakers bread called "Hillbilly Bread." We almost turned it down because of the "hillbilly" reference. A hillbilly will call himself a hillbilly, but he doesn't want someone else doing it or implying that he is one.

The latest *Pulse* figures available in Eugene show Radio KATR now *leads in total audience, total adult audience, total men audience in drive times, total women audience,* and *total drive time audience.*

This is a day of specialization in radio. With radio stations in every town and hamlet across the land, more are gathered in bunches at the larger cross roads. Radio KATR is strictly country & western in Eugene, Oregon—*they* like it, and *we* like it—all the way to the bank.

17

DALE PETERSON

Mr. Peterson has been in broadcasting since 1947. He has served as assistant to the president of KFWB and KFWB-FM from 1956 to 1959. In 1959 Mr. Peterson became general sales manager of KGBS, Los Angeles, California and in 1965 became general manager of that station.

IN 1965 over 100 radio stations, that were formerly playing some other form of music, converted to country music. *Sponsor Magazine* recently had this to say: "Country music is radio's hottest trend. Radio station managers and program directors attending the MacGavern Guild rep firm's two day programming seminar conceded that country music is radio's hottest trend, with the talk format running a close second."

What happened to give country and western music the sudden prominence it enjoys today?

First, let me say that the boots and saddles are gone. Fifteen to 20 years ago country music was a good, specialized business. There was very little research data available, and most national advertising agencies felt a country format generally deserved very little consideration.

Why did country music change?

Some years back, Shellby Singleton, who directed scores of

music sessions for Mercury Records, conducted a recording session in New York. As an experiment, he invited seven Nashville musicians to New York to record with a group of popular artists. Several important personages in the field of music were invited to the session "to see how it's done in Nashville." This was the beginning of the universality of the Nashville sound and modern country music.

Country music artists today use more instruments (the fiddles are gone). Violins, pianos and saxophones have been added; even the trumpet is sneaking in! The thin-wailing sound is all but gone.

Records, recorded by heretofore complete and total country artists, recorded with the Nashville sound, became hits in the pop field. In past months, we have seen Eddy Arnold, for instance, enjoy three giant records, equal hits in both the pop field and the country music field. Now Eddy Arnold didn't go down to the recording studio at RCA Victor in Nashville and say, "I'm going to cut a pop record; one that I know will go in the pop field, and also in the country field." Eddy Arnold went down to RCA Victor's recording studio in Nashville, and he and Chet Atkins, cut the best country record that they could possibly make. And, without a doubt, it was bound to be a hit in the pop field, too, because it was the best country record to come along. Country music is also patriotic . . . "Viet Nam Blues" by Dave Dudley, "Star Spangled Banner Waving Somewhere," plus many others, tell the story of our times. The shift of population to urban areas, the return to the city square, is a part of our life.

Like Mexican music, country music can also take a serious or sad song and put happy music behind it. Like a man born poor, who lives his entire life as a poor man, he learns to laugh at himself. Country music reflects life as it is.

The transference of artists to pop music from country music, and country music to pop, was a one way street. A country music artist could have a hit in the pop field, and many of them have—Marty Robbins, Jim Reeves, George Jones, Buck Owens, Eddy Arnold, Roger Miller and many, many more. All of these are country artists who have had big smash records in the country field. However, it was a one way street. Few, if any, of the pop artists had hits in the country field. This, itself, is now gradually changing. More and more, pop artists are leaning towards cutting records with a country flavor because they just seem to go over better. However, I personally feel that great and lasting country artists are born, not made. Some pop singers will make it, but few. The same "soul" you find in top-40 greats, is in country singers!

At KGBS we are very proud of the fact that Dean Martin, one of the regular listeners to our station, recently recorded a full album of nothing but country music. All were songs which he had heard while driving to and from the studios, and listening to KGBS. It's what we call the "modern Nashville sound in country music," variously referred to as the modern sound of country music, the Nashville sound, the country and western sound, etc.

To the question of why country music has become so big, the answer is simple. It's good, listenable music. It is done and performed by people who know what they are doing, who are professional and who understand the workings of the music, and who play to the people and not to each other.

The large country music radio audiences are proof that the Nashville sound in growing in prominence. Country and western record sales are spiraling at a faster rate than ever. According to *Business Week,* four out of every ten records sold are either pure country music or have had a tremendous country influence. In time, this will be six out of ten. For instance, Roger Miller, a Nashville-type music entertainer, is big enough to get five record industry sales awards for one single record.

Many large agencies have finally become aware of the effectiveness of country music. For years, country music was considered the stepchild of the radio industry. In the old days, the dyed-in-the-wool country music station felt it was not doing the correct job, or presenting country music in the correct manner, if the disc jockey on the air didn't talk about "sloppin' the hogs" . . . He had to be called either Tex, Hay Seed Jake or Cotton Eyed Joe. He had to talk in an accent that you could cut with a knife, and it was required, regardless of his education, that he use incorrect grammar.

The two-and-a-half minute hard sell pitches, the reference to neighbors sloppin' the hogs, the old hayseed manner are all things of the past.

Day by day, record companies are giving radio stations a better product to play. Today, the Nashville sound is bright, and these bright sounds earn high ratings and are rapidly winning more advertising acceptance.

18

JERRY GLASER

Mr. Glaser graduated from Vanderbilt University in 1954 and immediately went into radio as promotion manager and account executive of WLAC Radio. In 1958 he became general manager of a new country music station, WENO, Nashville, Tennessee. Currently Mr. Glaser serves on the board of directors of the Country Music Association.

FOR YEARS the terms "hillbilly" and "country music" were synonymous. That's all changed now, for the hillbilly of today is "pickin' and grinnin' " all the way to the bank, and we refer to him today as an artist.

The-on-the-air sound of the modern country and western broadcaster is backed up by livewire promotions and sharp merchandising that is bringing new dollars into the country music business. In Norfolk, Virginia, a gentleman by the name of George Crump not only is a very active member in his community's civic projects, but is active in promoting his station with on-the-air features that include *surfing reports, helicopter reports, reports from Nashville* each hour, and lively *contests* like his recent "gold brick contest" which awarded a listener a $500 Ft. Knox type gold brick.

In San Diego, California, an enterprising young broadcaster by the name of Dan McKinnon not only covers the local and national agencies with colorful eye-catching brochures, but also goes right to his listeners. In one of Dan's recent promotions, he flew his station's airplane over a nearby military survival course, dropped pamphlets, and offered any man who could escape the M.P.'s several hundred dollars worth of free records when he reached the station.

CFGM, Toronto is one of Canada's finest country and western stations and has proved it has the listeners with their "country club," which has over 50,000 registered members. The members not only get special prizes, but have an opportunity to get special buys on various advertisers products, which has turned out to be an *excellent form of national merchandising.*

In Houston, Texas, recently a country music station worked in conjunction with the annual boat show and surprised even themselves when over 30,000 people showed up to watch a country music show in the Astrodome.

If you were to visit Nashville, Tennessee, you'd find it's not uncommon to see 2,000 people jammed into a shopping center to watch WENO Radio's famous "Country A-Go-Go" road show, complete with a swinging western band, gaily painted stage, and the WENO A-Go-Go girls, gyrating on the stage. By the way, WENO's annual Easter Egg Hunt, on the WENO Ranch near Nashville pulled over 30,000 people this year.

The story of successful country and western broadcasting goes on and on, and you can find success stories in markets from Los Angeles to New York and from El Paso to Toronto. The success I might add, isn't limited to radio. Alert television station owners are finding country music can mean both ratings, and advertising dollars to their station. Over 30 shows are being seen each week coast to coast.

In Atlanta, Georgia, a syndicated c & w show, slotted in a late Saturday afternoon time period, pulls a higher rating than any other show on the station, except *Peyton Place,* and if we can figure a way to add a little more sex to a five string banjo, I think we can beat that show, also.

Not only syndicated country shows are on the increase, but network shows as well. Producers and directors have been getting their feet wet in the country music water, little by little, and in 1966 we've seen Eddy Arnold on the *Bell Telephone Hour,* Roger Miller on his own special, Ferlin Husky on the Merv Griffin show, and Little Jimmy Dickens on *Hullabaloo.*

Not only broadcasters, but top agencies as well, are taking a second look at the "hayseed sound" and finding that country music is a force that can make the cash register ring. You'll find agencies like Gardner, D'Arcy, and William Esty placing regular business on country music stations, and blue chip accounts like Pet Milk, R. J. Reynolds, Coca Cola, and Kellogg's placing thousands and thousands of dollars every day on country music stations. We know that most agency people won't buy a concept of any kind without a few numbers, or statistics to back it up. And that's just what we've got.

A very experienced gentleman on the West Coast by the name of Dick Schofield found he was in need of information to take to his agency friends in the L.A. market, and since none were available, he arranged for a demographic survey of California listeners. The results made timebuyers sit up and take notice. The Country Music Association arranged for a *Pulse* survey of the same type last year, in over 20 U.S. markets and the facts are official. C and w market penetration went as high as 48%. Medium income was $5,675, with 5% making *over* $10,000 a year. Seventy-five percent of the listeners owned their own homes; 31% of the households owned two cars; 70.6% has at least one savings account (meaning they had at least a little excess money each year); the average age was 45 years.

WJJD, Chicago, went a step further and engaged a firm to make a demographic study of the WJJD audience. The results are real eye-openers. Among the facts they learned about the WJJD country listeners were: 8% were professional (doctors, lawyers, teachers, technical); 7% were managerial (executives, managers, supervisors); 15% were clerical and sales; 23% were skilled and semi-skilled; 13% were unskilled; 3% students, or in the military; 8% were blue collar female; 21% were housewives. Other brief facts . . . 30% owned two cars, 45% owned their own homes; 23% of the WJJD listeners make between $7,500 and $10,000 a year, 64% own an FM radio.

WJJD has one of the finest success stories in C & W Radio. In the latest ratings, WJJD had moved into the position of one of the top four stations in Chicago. Today WJJD is making waves in a market where before it hardly made a ripple. WJJD's parent company, Plough, Inc., is so sold on the country music story that it recently changed another of its stations, WPLO in Atlanta, to full time country music. Not only Plough, but other large independent operators and groups are getting on the country and western bandwagon. Storer Broadcasting has begun broadcasting full time c & w in Los Angeles with their KGBS. WWVA in Wheeling, West Virginia, WJRZ in Newark, New Jersey, and WTHE in Long Island, New York, have all picked up the modern country music sound and the ratings to go with it.

I'm happy to say than in many markets c & w is a real force to be reckoned with. In Sacramento, in early 1966, KRAK Radio, a full time 50,000 watt country and Western giant, moved into the top spot in the daytime *Pulse* ratings. From 6 A.M. until 6 P.M. each day, KRAK leads the race in a highly competitive market.

The old weather-beaten image that country music is the squeaky fiddle and the nasal announcer broadcasting for the exclusive consumption of the backwoodsman is as archaic as high button shoes. Today over 300 stations program c & w full time. Four hundred program at least six hours a day or more, and 500 stations program at least three hours a day. In addition, I might add we're all watching with interest a television station in Oklahoma City, that recently went *all* country. And so it goes. And as the listener goes, more and more so will go the advertiser.

PART FIVE

"Beautiful" Music

19. F. Geer Parkinson
    Vice President and Station Manager, WRYT, Pittsburgh, Penn.

20. Wally Nelskog
    President and General Manager, KIXI, Seattle, Washington

21. Gil Bond
    General Sales Manager, KIXI, Seattle, Washington.

There are a lot of different names for it—sweet music, conservative music, good music or, as I have elected to call it in this section, "beautiful" music—which, incidentally, seems to be the most common term for this type of modern radio format.

Beautiful music ranges in style on certain of America's radio stations from sweet pops to light classics, with strong emphasis on standards and Broadway musicals.

Usually on most beautiful music radio stations, the music is carefully paced in accordance with the time of day and the activities of the listener.

A great many beautiful music stations are winning top ratings in major markets across the country. In this section, three beautiful music specialists from large cities in different parts of the country tell how they've built successful stations from this unusual type of program format.

19

F. GEER PARKINSON

A veteran of more than 30 years in the broadcasting industry, Mr. Parkinson is a native of Columbus, Ohio, where he was graduated from the School of Journalism of Ohio State University. He is currently vice president and station manager of WRYT Radio in Pittsburgh, Pennsylvania. He has held this position with WYRT and its predecessor WCAE since 1958.

IF YOU ARE A young old-timer, you probably remember Titus Moody. Mr. Moody was a resident of "Allen's Alley," one of the mainstays of the Fred Allen radio program. When once queried by Fred Allen as to the virtues of a certain radio program, Titus Moody, a hayseed philosopher, leveled Mr. Allen and the industry generally with the reply: "I don't know nothin' 'bout radio. Far as I'm concerned, I hold no trust with a piece of talkin' furniture."

Well, radio has always been much more than a piece of talking furniture—in the 1930s *and* today. The content and method of radio programming has changed through the years and now we have a more fragmentized concept—that is to say, more specific programming for more specific audiences. In the Pittsburgh market we found a specific audience void, and we filled it with WRYT and beautiful music.

What is beautiful music? Beautiful music is music with a flowing, well-defined melody line. Music that is memorable—that one can hum and sing to, music that has passed the test of time. As one Pittsburgh columinist said, "Music that one can read and *WRYT* to." In fact, it's grown-up music for grown-up people.

WRYT began May 28, 1961 as an outgrowth of WCAE, a prominent property in Pittsburgh broadcasting for almost 40 years. The change of call letters from WCAE to WRYT was minor compared to the sharp change in programming policy. We had struggled, in vain, since 1958 to compete with two very successful "top 40" stations. Realizing the existence of an important audience which was being frustrated by the dissonance of sounds emanating from most other Pittsburgh stations, we decided to make a complete break with past programming. Hence, beautiful WRYT music was born.

Music is the primary key to WRYT programming. Our musical format is as precise as any "contemporary" music station. It ranges in style from sweet pops to light classics, with strong emphasis on standards and Broadway musicals. The variety is categorized and programmed continuously on a 15-minute basis. Every selection aired by WRYT is auditioned by a qualified music librarian. WRYT music is carefully paced in accordance with the time of day and the activities of the listener. The early morning is characterized by many up-tempoed, lift selections—going into the housewife hours from 9 A.M. until 3 P.M., creating a quieter mood, interspersed with some familiar light classics. On into the afternoon traffic period, the music is up-tempoed, not as lively as the morning period but livelier than the daytime musical selections. Then the music is gradually softened into the evening hours where a "soft lights and sweet music" atmosphere is created on into the night and until the wake-up hours in the morning.

Play list selections are chosen for their familiarity and brilliance. The quiet background sounds are minimized, and only the best arrangements are acceptable. The main task in building a beautiful music format is to make non-raucous music exciting and interesting—a thing in and of itself, not merely a backdrop of half-listening activity. I have often thought, in looking impersonally at our format, that what we have created is a truly good music station with a contemporary format super-imposed upon it, to build the station into a foreground vehicle—not a background Muzak.

Our commercial format is basic to the industry now, and we are in what is commonly known as "the cluster system." In brief, a continuous flow of music over a 12-minute period with news in a cluster on the hour, a three-commercial cluster on the quarter-after, half and quarter-of the hour—12 commercials in all. At no time do we double-spot. Between every commercial is a spot-breaker, which may be time, weather, civic activities, exotics, special promotions or contests.

We admit, with justifiable pride, that our soft-sell "gimmicks" have been highly successful. Some are so subtle that the audience doesn't know whether it's being kidded or not. Others are more directly and intentionally obvious. Pittsburgh listeners of WRYT have been enticed with frequent exotic commercials, contests and special promotions.

Several Christmases ago, audiences were urged to buy parakeet pants for the "parakeet who has everything." Another item offered was a do-it-yourself whirlybird to help ease downtown traffic congestion. One of our most unusual was a Christmas offering designed to attract the attention of the youngsters.

Another exotic was WRYT's endeavor to capture the imagination of the gourmet with a new approach to break the monotony of the traditional Thanksgiving dinner. We offered the recipe that has long been a Thanksgiving favorite with Bedouin tribes. Over 1800 requests came in for the stuffed camel, and each request was filled with the actual recipe. Another culinary item, elephant stew, was recommended the following Christmas. It takes three months to prepare and serves 3,860 guests.

We have conducted many special station promotions, the most successful of which was the "Teenage Underground." Fred Remington of *The Pittsburgh Press* wrote that WRYT would rather have the antenna melted down and made into paper clips than play rock and roll. WRYT made its bid for the juvenile audience. A series of 16 different announcements were used over a period of six weeks climaxed by a parade and special meeting of the "teenage underground" at a local theatre during which time Dr. William Steinberg, conductor of the Pittsburgh Symphony Orchestra became the "Commanding General of the teenage underground armies." Four thousand teenagers turned out for the parade and meeting.

We continually strive to inject into our format subtle humor which can work in a good music format, and it performs an obvious and vital function. It keeps people talking about WRYT. Promotions, both on and off the air are a continuing effort. The station uses all available media on a regularly scheduled basis. When we first took off, we even purchased the sign-off announcements on two local radio stations to promote our own nighttime broadcasts.

We have a firm belief that a responsible radio station should promote the communities in its coverage area. WRYT does just that. Every quarter-hour in our broadcast day is introduced by what we commonly call a "mood intro." It may be a one or two liner which calls attention to the current progress, history, the vitality and the many other attributes of the Pittsburgh city. In addition, special messages are aired daily calling attention to the beauty and pleasures of western Pennsylvania life and to the area's civic and industrial achievements.

Business, civic and religious leaders are singled out and honored every day with a salute from WRYT for their contributions to the community, prompting one local columnist to refer to the station as a "24-hour a day Chamber of Commerce." These salutes have a two-fold purpose. Not only do they build community well-being, but get individual names on the air. Also, in our spot breakers are non-commercial announcements which play heavily on cultural events, music, art, books, concerts, ballet, etc.

There are many general programming facets that add to WRYT's success. The station believes in an absolute minimum of talk from announcers. All non-essential information is eliminated— no small talk or prattling deejays. A short harp-bridge is placed between each selection. The sound of the harp-bridge is an "audio sig cut" for WRYT. Every time this sound is heard, the listener knows his dial is set at 1250 or WRYT. In the total sound, this uncluttered yet free-flowing quality attunes the listener's ear to the spoken word and makes commercials more effective while it enhances the pleasure of listening.

As manager of WRYT, I feel that conservative music can and—unquestionably in the case of WRYT—does pay off. In 1965, we enjoyed our highest profit in recent history. The first quarter of 1966 showed an additional gain of 5% over 1965's beautiful music —which only goes to show that you can do wonders with a piece of talking furniture.

20

WALLY NELSKOG

Educated at the Cornish School of Fine Arts, Seattle, Washington and Yale University, Mr. Nelskog has been involved in ownership and operation of radio stations in Washington, Oregon, California, Montana and North Dakota. He founded KIXI, Seattle in 1961 and is now vice president and general manager of that station.

OUR KIXI success story is basically a sturdy and lasting structure of bricks and mortar, fashioned for Seattle's *prime market* of adults —the ones who are 21 to 50 years old and enjoy higher incomes. These people don't want to be jingled to death. They don't want the nervous din of fast-paced commercials, rock and roll jingles and low-brow humor. Such commercial devices are offensive to the KIXI audience. Neither will the KIXI listener tolerate a sound of one special feature after another all day and all night long . . . which reminds me of the two wrong types of program director situations so common today.

On the one hand, we have the under-paid program director who works endless hours creating "cute" features by the bushel just to show his station manager that he is working very hard . . . and he deserves a raise. The other extreme, and equally bad, is the over-paid program director who works and works to create the same kind of "audience-chaser-awayers" to show that he's *worth* his salary.

What we need today—especially for the KIXI kind of good music station—are mature, expert, experienced program directors who understand the sensibilities and desires of a prime-market audience of better-educated, higher-income adults, 25 to 50 years old. This program director must have the feeling for a "total sound" that is made up of two absolutely necessary ingredients . . . which I like to call "bricks and mortar."

You ask: "What is a 'brick'?" Each cut of a long playing record, each song or instrumental, each newscast, each commercial, each and every element of your music, your information, these are the "bricks" that will build a beautiful, lasting structure of programming—or if they're the wrong kind of *bricks,* a very temporary structure that will not endure in the rating books.

The "mortar"—the stuff that binds your bricks together—is for "color," for texture, for strength and durability . . . identification mood setters, pacers, station promos, public service. The "mortar" will *condition* your choice of the right bricks into a complete, beautiful package of sound—a formula that only succeeds from its total dimensions. It's the "total sound" that distinguishes KIXI from all other Seattle stations. You cannot identify a "good-music" station or a "better-music" station in a market unfamiliar to your experience by looking at a music list, by examining the length and number of newscasts. You must have listened to the station—to its selection and sequence of bricks—to the mortar which levens the sound. And don't forget that the real back-bone of a good or better music station, is the music.

If you asked me to describe KIXI's music in one word I'd say, "bright." Bright is a creed with us. Bright and up-tempo in traffic times . . . bright and smooth during the day . . . bright and beautiful for evening. The hot, new, adult tunes are pre-programed on our hot tape, and punched into the program regularly—two or three times an hour—thus keeping the immediate, the current always brightly up-front.

Always keep your commercial acceptance department alert! Be just as selective with your commercials as you are with your music, lest you give the wrong impression of how you sound. Never *offend* the ear you're selling. We have redone many national spots that were undesirable to our particular audience . . . with permission, of course. Programming and sales must work together in harmony to get maximum dollars from advertisers.

21

GIL BOND

Educated at Ohio and Harvard Universities, Mr. Bond for many years was an instructor of English. He entered the broadcasting field in 1947 as general manager of KVSM, San Mateo, California. He joined KIXI, Seattle, Washington, November 1, 1963 in his present position of general sales manager.

WHETHER your program-product is "country & western," "classical," "talk," or "middle-of-the-road music with personalities," the challenge to program directors is very different today from yesterday. Have you, the program director, begun thinking about your product in terms of marketing objectives? Are you, sales managers, discussing with your program directors today's new requirements for making sales—such specifics as age, income, family life cycle, listeners per household, blue-collar or white-collar, etc.?

The day before yesterday the programming-sales success was evaluated in terms of over-all share of homes. Yesterday we needed only gross rating points to make the sale. Last night the emphasis shifted to gross men, women or adults or teens. Up to this point a program director only had to deliver a sufficient *quantity* in the right category. If the station's revenue didn't hit an all-time high, the sales manager was playing too much golf or spending too much time in the local bar.

Then came today's profit squeeze with a re-evaluation of

advertising expenditures . . . in terms of new information via the computer. Suddenly time-buyers and marketing men are asking this searching question: How does *your* listener-market profile match *my* product profile? Today every station's audience is being judged by increasingly sophisticated *qualitative* standards. The wide-awake broadcaster knows that he can no longer seek rating dominance in numbers by being "all-things-to-all-people." He must select an audience target and program to it.

In marketing KIXI to advertisers (both local and national) we sell a "three-part" *spectrum*. We sell KIXI as "standing alone" at the quality end of the Seattle spectrum. We suggest the inclusion of one station, from a group of three, from the opposite end of the spectrum. (Two of these are top-40 and one is country & western.) To complete the buy we suggest one station from the middle group, which we call "middle-of-the-road and personality." There are four stations in this middle group, three of which are network affiliates and one independent. Our theme is: *"In Seattle, It Takes Three To Cover The Spectrum."* This is the advertisement which we always run in *Standard Rate and Data Service* and sometimes in other trade publications.

In the beginning, KIXI picked a spot in the Seattle spectrum of station formats—between the classical music station and the "middle-of-the-roaders"—and succeeded in drawing substantial audience from both sides. This accounts for the term "better music" rather than "good music."

The key to our success—or to your proposed success—in programming beautiful music, good music, or better music, is in defining the range of our music and the variations within this range, for specific segments of your broadcast day. If you succeed, you will not be directly competitive with any other station in your market . . . especially if you maintain your partnership between programming and sales.

If your "beautiful market" is "top-40-contemporary," be proud to sell it. Don't be ashamed of an adult audience almost half of which is 18-24 years old. Again, if your "beautiful music" is country & western, don't be abashed by your predominently "blue-collar" audience. These very young adults, these blue-collar adults, are very often just as important to an advertiser as the KIXI "white-collar, higher-income" adult.

If you feel that you are treading water, why not re-examine the station spectrum in your market and decide for yourself where your best opportunity lies. The *Pulses, Mediastats* and *ARBs* for various other markets will give you a rough idea of the audience-market characteristics for your proposed new role in your community. And when you achieve your "first-place" position—whether it be in young adults or middle-aged adults, in medium- or higher-income homes, in homes with more people, or in homes ranking high in children or teens—be forthright in selling your strong points. Your sales dollars will grow and grow.

Certainly the way we *sell* our "first-place" positions, our strong points, will affect the image of the station we represent. I like to think of the word "image" as the total reflection of a radio station in its community of listeners and advertisers. So we must ask ourselves: "Are we thinking in terms of a *small* image, or are we working every day to expand the good image of the station we represent?"

PART SIX

FM Radio

22. LYNN A. CHRISTIAN
    General Manager, WPIX-FM, New York, N.Y.

23. ROBERT BRUTON
    Program Director, WFAA Radio, Dallas, Texas

24. EVERETT B. COBB
    General Manager, KNEV, Reno, Nevada

As long as I can remember in this wonderful—but sometimes exasperating—world of FM radio, everyone talks about change. Prosperity has always been "just around the corner." Everyone with the remotest connection to FM radio has been wondering for these many years, which corner? Will FM make it?

Today it's crystal clear that the FM scene has definitely changed. FM radio is, indeed, radio and has become a major force in broadcasting. One can see it in increased set sales, mass coverage and penetration. You can see it in cash flow and new advertising dollars. And some can see it in profits. It's now allowed that there is a substantial unduplicated FM audience.

The price differential between AM only and FM and AM on a radio set today is negligible. It is now possible to get an AM-FM receiver for as little as $9.98, and lower prices are still in the offing.

In this section, three of the nation's most respected FM broadcasters tell how they're programming—each in his own way—to the growing numbers of FM listeners. Each station supplies a different need in each market, and each station manager tells how he, first of all, learned what those needs were, and then how he proceeded to build a program schedule on his FM station geared to fill them.

22

LYNN A. CHRISTIAN

As general manager of WPIX-FM, the full time stereo station of the New York *Daily News,* Mr. Christian joined the new station four months prior to its going on the air in October, 1964. Before that time, he was general manager of KODA and KODA-FM, two separately programmed good music stations in Houston, Texas. He is a 1953 graduate of the University of Houston and also attended Emerson College in Boston.

FIRST, just in case you didn't know it, you can have a whale of a lot of fun in FM radio. Note I did not say FM. Let there be no confusion. FM in my book is FM *radio*. FM is what a lot of confused, non-broadcast type people in advertising agencies, at old fashioned trade publications, hi-fi magazines have been calling our finest radio dial.

FM radio is a happening, and FM stereo radio is like no other. Tinted tubes to the contrary, it is the greatest thing that ever happened to broadcasting. And if it has not yet happened to most broadcasters, I'm sorry. During the past five years, nearly 600 new FM stations have gone on the air, and over 25 million new FM-equipped receivers have been sold to listen to them.

Just a fad? The "in" thing?

Let me tell you about a couple of stations that decided a few years ago to jump in with both feet. One is down in Houston. Dave Morris has been running a swinging rock and roll (contemporary) music AM station called KNUZ for many years. One day he decided he wanted to join in the fun. He got a construction permit for an FM station. And he programmed it with bright, good music, top news coverage, limited talk—and all in stereo. He called his new radio station KQE. It became popular, audience-wise immediately —an audience, too, that he had not been getting on his AM radio station.

Suddenly, he not only had two sets of expenses, he also had a pair of unduplicated audiences and two lovely sets of profit figures. It almost goes without saying that his two stations, combined, earned a larger total share of the entire Houston market.

Isolated case? Luck? Nonsense. Dave Morris is a fierce competitor and was during my 1958 to 1964 FM management trek at KODA-FM in Houston. He saw an opportunity, and he fielded it beautifully. In a recent study, his FM radio station had a third as much total audience as his AM radio station, which is sold out much of the time. Sounds like income security—the kind my insurance man is always pitching.

Never happen again? How about WSB-FM in Atlanta? Elmo Ellis' AM station and his separately programmed FM radio station are both ranked among the top five stations in the total Atlanta radio market. Then there's WMAL-FM in Washington and KIXL-FM in Dallas and WABC-FM in New York and KIBW-FM in Wichita and dozens more. Or, how about Garrett Allen's separately programmed country-western money-maker in Statesville, North Carolina (WFMX)?

It is happening all over the nation. When a knowledgable broadcaster decides to plunge into FM radio with a full commitment to program separately with new ideas, to seek new audiences, he comes up with a Dave Morris or Garrett Allen success story. But forget about partial commitments. That's the road to listener schizophrenia. And if no one else in your organization will tell you, I will. Sellers of automation equipment and syndicated programming paint a beautiful low-cost story. But you show me an FM radio station, which has two separate program images in the course of any given day, and I'll show you a quick way to ease your tax burden. Your FM radio station should not compete with your AM radio station. And your AM radio salesmen should not be attempting to sell time on your FM radio station. Your FM radio station should have a separate identity beginning with its call letters, continuing with its promotion, and especially with its on air staff.

This sounds like a bright Alice-in-Wonderland story of fame and fortune in a medium that did a whopping $20 million in total sales in 1964 according to the FCC. Granted, there are plenty of FM radio stations losing money. However, at this very same stage in AM radio's early years, the percentage of loss was even higher. And the sale of FM radio receivers far exceeds a comparable period in AM radio history.

Program decisions are strictly of a local nature. For the operator of an independent FM radio station in New York City to tell anyone how to program in Springfield, Harrisburg, Tampa or Roanoke, would be committing a gross error. However, I do feel obligated to tell you a little about our station. It was sort of a happening. Charlie Whitaker and I came up to Big Town from KODA in Houston. Charlie's my program director and long time friend and associate. We were in awe of New York. We listened to William B. and Goodman Ace and Junior John Gambling and Barry Gray and many more. We were slightly puzzled. New York AM radio sounded awfully talky. New York FM radio sounded awfully dull. We knew that WPAT had the conservative music listener, and a sharecropper from Oklahoma could have spotted WQXR's dominance in the classical format field. WNEW appeared leaning to more contemporary music, and WNBC, WOR and WCBS were engaged in a verbal war. WABC, WINS and WMCA had the swingers locked up. So we decided to program to the young adult group.

In our not so humble opinions, there really was not one FM radio station in New York programming consistently to younger men and women 20 to 40 on a 24-hour basis. So Charlie developed the PIX-Mix—a nine-part formula with stereo goodies for everyone. We liked it. And we felt that it went with today's good life—enjoyed by the millions in our vast urban area. So we called it "The Sound of the Good Life." And since our station is on the 28th floor of the Daily News Building, with a terrace view of Manhattan, we called our studios "The Pix Penthouse."

We added a small but professional announcing staff, developed a complete hourly news service (5 min. before the hour), enlisted a sales organization (the hardest task), created a Charter advertising package for just seven advertisers and proceeded to sell them. And advertisers begot advertisers, like: Pan American Airways, Newport Cigarettes, Delta Airlines, First National City Bank, Arnold Bread, Blue Cross, Equitable Assurance, Coty Perfume, American Express, Renault-Peugeot, Macy's, Mazola, New York Telephone, Iberia Airlines, Savings Banks of New York, Trans World Airlines, B. Altman's, National Van Lines, Alitalia Airlines, Squibb, Cinzano Vermouth, Bulova, Pepperidge Farms Soups, Cantrece Nylon, Citroen, Grace Lines, First Federal Savings, Sylvania, Kent Cigarettes and Ford Motor Co. But we do miss local advertisers in Big Town. Try to identify a radio station at the corner of East 42nd Street and 2nd Avenue in the heart of Manhattan with a local drug store or a local car dealer or a local anything!

That's the PIX-FM story. And thanks to a consistent program sound, excellent promotion, and a lot of hard work by a relatively small staff of 14 full and part-time people, we have been able to realize a substantial audience in just 18 months on the air. The January/February 1966 New York ARB Radio Study indicates that we have attracted the largest unduplicated weekly audience ever accorded to a separately programmed FM radio station in any market by any rating service. As a solid base to grow on, we are understandably proud of this early achievement.

So what makes a "happening" happen? It's a combination of different elements which on the surface appear to be going in separate directions, but which, in reality, flow together to build a complete unity of thought and purpose. (Or anyway, that's how Salvador Dali explained it at Lincoln Center.)

The elements in our "happening" are these:

Continuous Growth of FM Radio Set Sales

Witness the report from the Electronics Industries Association for the first quarter of 1966, following on the heels of a spectacular 1965—which was 35% ahead of 1964. For 1966 the EIA had predicted an increase of another 28%. However, if the first quarter is any indicator, it now appears that *over 11 million* FM-equipped radios—domestic and imported—will have been sold in 1966! The reason? Domestic sale of FM receivers is up, not by 28%, but rather by 47% over the first quarter of 1965 as indicated below.

	First Quarter 1965	First Quarter 1966
FM Table, Portable & Clock Radios	655,000	1,031,000
Hi-Fi, Stereo Phono/FM Combo	322,000	370,000
Color TV/FM Combo	27,000	95,000
Portable Phono/FM	13,000	15,000
Auto FM	131,000	172,000

The low priced radios are up by 57% and the car FM's are up by 31%. At this rate *one out of every three radios* sold in America in 1966—domestic and imported—will have been *FM-equipped*. This compares to one out of every nine in 1960.

Improved Research and rating Techniques

FM home and auto penetration figures from Hooper were due in the summer of 1966 in a special study made for Quality Media, Inc., the national FM sales representative firm. Pulse breakouts of separately programmed FM stations began with July 1966 studies. Unduplicated audience studies by ARB and Mediastat will show what percentage of FM radio audiences listens to leading AM stations.

FM Car Radio's Momentum

The concentrated efforts by the National Association of FM Broadcasters and its member stations to encourage FM radio listeners to put FM alongside their AM on the road as well as in the home are producing excellent results. General Motors announced that FM *stereo* radios were available for almost every model of its 1967 line. There are FM radios, custom or under dash, for virtually every make and model automobile—imported or domestic. FM/AM car radios are available with the Lear Jet Stereo Cartridge tape playbacks in many major lines. An increasing number of stations are adding vertical polarization to their transmission to improve and completely stabilize FM car radio reception via its normal vertical antenna mounting.

New Program Concepts and Syndication Services

Out of the 1,466 FM radio stations licensed in the U.S., including the educational stations, 826 are now programmed and sold separately. Many of these stations are experimenting to develop new audiences to FM, such as KLZ-FM in Denver. This Time-Life station is a hard-rock FM station every morning and evening, and on weekends. Manager Lee Fondren notes that it is doing so well that he soon intends to separate the entire day from his middle-of-the-road AM station. At WSDM in Chicago, and at WNEW-FM in New York, the ladies will be running the turntables. Gordon McClendon has high hopes for making his Los Angeles FM'er an all-classified ad station, and there's a lot of national interest on the outcome of this application. WLS-FM, the ABC owned station in Chicago, programs live sports every night it's available—and in stereo. KBRG in San Francisco has gone from classical to all ethnic. Then there's Walter Windsor's new FM in Lubbock, Texas. He got a license to program 100% entertainment—and aren't we all just a little green with envy?

The new CBS-FM Program Service, called the "Young Sound," went on the air over their owned-FM stations in Fall, 1966. Bill Greene, who has developed this concept, is also offering it on a syndicated service basis which is certainly an interesting approach for FM radio. Meanwhile, other program syndicators with a wide variety of types of service include: The Triangle Audio Program Service, with six different types of service: Musicpac, an all-stereo custom music service; IGM, one of the pioneers in syndication; and Prologue, a stereo music service currently being used by Metromedia FM stations.

And some of the biggest news in the way of networking comes from ABC, where Alex Smallens reports that satellite transmission of FM stereo will be available on a coast-to-coast basis within the next five to ten years. At NBC, it is reported that a classical music program service is being prepared in Cleveland to be broadcast on their owned-FM stations.

Advancing Values of FM Radio Properties

A major broadcast broker told me following the 1966 FM meetings in Chicago that FM property values increased by up to $50,000 in major markets immediately following those encouraging sessions. Stations in Chicago, Los Angeles and San Francisco are selling for over $400,000, and WRFM in New York was purchased for $850,000 by the Mormon Church.

The FM Radio Broadcaster's Interest in His Industry

It may come as a shock to some, but as of May, 1966 69% of all of the FM radio stations on the air in America were members of the NAB, while only 55% of the AM stations belonged. I say this only to bury once and for all the old theory that FM station operators were non-broadcasters who were not interested in supporting industry policy as established by the NAB.

That's the FM "happening." In closing I would like you to read this short paragraph:

"During about a two-decade history of FM broadcasting, many knowledgeable and influential broadcasters and manufacturers have earnestly predicted that FM would die on the vine. Many of these same people have subtly fought FM. They had their reasons, which we need not go into, but in the main it was because FM development would adversely affect their profits or equalize the opportunity of their competitors in the market place. But FM did not die on the vine. It has had some setbacks and close calls, but it has survived like a cat with nine lives. It has survived because it is too good a thing to kill off. It is good for all but a handful of high-powered AM stations, because FM coverage is vastly greater day and night. It is good for the listener because the signal is reliable and its quality of reception is infinitely better. FM radio has survived and progressed, because it has offered a service, which has become a symbol of quality. I urge you to keep it a symbol of quality." That was Commissioner Robert Bartley's comment in 1963.

But remember, too, it can be a lot of fun.

23

ROBERT BRUTON

Robert Bruton recently was program manager of WFAA AM-FM, Dallas-Fort Worth, Texas. His broadcasting career began at KXOL, Fort Worth, while he was still in high school. He later became production manager and program director of that station as well as operations advisor for the Wendell Mayes Group, which included KXOL, KNOW, Austin, Texas and KTOK, Oklahoma City. Mr. Bruton joined WFAA as assistant program director in 1964.

FM HAS MOST definitely arrived—and for a very good reason. For the first time, we as broadcasters have been forced to look at this very effective medium for what it is—*radio*. It is not "an automated jukebox," a background service or cultural mecca. It is plain dollars-and-sense *radio*.

In the summer of 1965 WFAA Radio began to consider several alternatives to the FCC 50% non-duplication ruling for dual AM-FM outlets. Minimum compliance versus complete separation and live versus automation were some of the things considered and how they would affect service to our audience. Since WFAA, Dallas and WBAP, Fort Worth share time on the 570 and 820 frequencies, our FM service was the only continuity we had to our programming. Cost and revenue factors, naturally, entered into our advanced planning. We found there was little cost differential between live and automation operations except—and this was a big except—within five years automation would pay for itself, whereas a live operation was a continuous cost factor that would increase rather than decrease over the years.

In the fall of 1965, the decision was reached to completely separate programming and operate WFAA-FM as a self-sustaining station. The staff was to be limited to a manager-salesman, one salesman, a secretary (continuity, traffic, sales secretary) and a production man to nursemaid the automation equipment. Regardless of what the brochures will tell you, it still takes people to operate even the most sophisticated machines. In the case of WFAA-FM, Shafer automated system with six music playbacks, two time machine playbacks, one spotter commercial and a Collins tape deck plus two automatic program loggers were chosen. This we found is a minimum amount of program equipment and does not include production support equipment, which consists of a full size control room capable of going on the air if necessary, plus the Shafer "makeup" machine and its related controls. All music is preselected to fit a prescribed format and is recorded by our AM announcers. Production support is furnished by AM but all talent used is charged back to FM.

After determining the needs of our audience, through special research, it was necessary to formulate these wants into a saleable sound. At present there are several excellent FM stations in Dallas programming background type of music. On WFAA it was decided the sound would be a foreground type of programming, so as to command the attention of the listener, without his realizing it, thus making him more attentive and receptive to commercial announcements. At WFAA-FM news is programmed at :15 past the hour with weather at :45 past. Our research proved the listener preferred little or no talk, farm or discussion type programs. Ninety-two percent of our programming is pure entertainment. All music is back or pre-announced; the time is given six times per hour, and during peak listener periods, this is increased to eight times per hour. We carry a maximum of six commercials, promotion and public service announcements per hour. Every other song is an instrumental and the entire station is programmed to a *medium* to *up* tempo beat with just a hint of the lush sound.

But, evolving this sound was only part of the job, since this was a totally new sound concept for Dallas. After six months of operation, WFAA-FM showed a profit and as of the latest Hooper and ARB rating books, is the number two FM station in Dallas. There is still room for improvement, in both profit and ratings. We have found that although automation is flexible, the immediacy of selling radio makes it almost impossible to continue without a live staff. Automation has given us the ratings and the revenues to prove to us that FM *has arrived* and, like Topsy, will grow and grow and grow if the industry will let it.

24

EVERETT B. COBB

Born in Massachusetts, Mr. Cobb first entered radio in 1924. After varied experience, including work on original television and as an air-personality on WISN, Milwaukee, Wisconsin, he moved to Reno, Nevada in 1938. In 1953, he established station KNEV-FM.

It really was not until advertising could be sold by radio stations that radio began to rival other sources of information. Radio has come a long way in three decades. Improved programming and broadcast facilities have, in great measure, been responsible for the incredible strides forward the industry has made in its comparatively short life.

In 1935, when Dr. Armstrong first demonstrated that a way had been found to eliminate static and noise from the broadcasting of radio programs, the first step forward in FM radio was noted. When the FCC started licensing FM stations, it was a second major step forward in radio broadcasting. By that time, however, hundreds of thousands of owners of radio sets were dependent almost entirely on AM radio and did not realize the improved broadcast methods that made FM easier on the ears, gave it a more true natural tone and improved the reception in the home.

FM radio broadcasting arrived in Reno, where KNEV went on the air, without much fanfare on Christmas Day, 1953. Before the station was established a survey was made and it was determined that there were many sets which could receive FM, but these were idle because there was no FM outlet in Nevada. These sets represented a worth of about one-half million dollars, and they could only become useful to the owners if there was a station broadcasting in FM. Another survey, taken shortly after we started, indicated that more than 28% of the homes were listening to KNEV, and a year later still another survey showed that almost 39% were steady listeners. We discovered in that survey that FM went straight up the social and economic scale, and by 1955 we had a 50% saturation. FM radio sets began to sell, and our dealers discovered a quarter of a million dollar market for radio sets they did not realize existed. Since then the demand for FM sets has increased by leaps and bounds, in the home, in cars, in business establishments . . . in fact in all walks of life.

KNEV, when it went on the air, was truly a pile of junk, for there was neither the money to buy new equipment, nor was new equipment available. Today, KNEV is an established business, and we have received many flattering offers to sell the station. KNEV has operated for 12 years without a sales department. Eighty percent of its advertisers have been on the air day after day for more than five years. Fifty percent have been on the air more than eight years, and some of them have been on the air since our first broadcast on Christmas Day, 1953.

KNEV's programming is out of the ordinary. Never has the station run a singing commercial, never has it played rock and roll. Never has it played a commercial that was loud and screaming. From the beginning it was felt that KNEV's appeal would be to those who liked good music, who wanted quiet entertainment and who found relaxation in what we were broadcasting. Now this may not be the accepted or popular appeal of radio, but for KNEV it has paid off.

Perhaps this type of programming would not be possible on an AM station. Perhaps it requires a special type of audience, but that audience is available in every section of the nation. Within KNEV's sphere of listeners are miners, farmers, Indians and people who are seeking to recover Nevada's mineral wealth in remote sections of the state. They have found KNEV helpful, educational, relaxing and informative. KNEV steers away from the sensational, both in subject and presentation. KNEV's programming is not all "highbrow." Popular music is used from Broadway productions, operettas and, in season, grand opera. Stereophonic sound is KNEV's greatest asset.

The average AM program, broadcast on FM, would not succeed any more than the FM programs could be successfully used on AM radio. *The Wall Street Journal* and the *Christian Science Monitor* do not have the popular appeal of the *Seattle Post Intelligence* or the *Seattle Times,* but both of these papers are doing exceptionally well. They have a special reader appeal just as FM radio has a special appeal, if it is properly programmed for the type of audience it attracts. Insofar as AM and FM radio are concerned, each fills a specific niche in the field of communication, of entertainment, and of information. There is room for both. The heavy investment in AM radio makes it unlikely that FM radio will supersede it, but that does not alter the fact that FM radio is definitely a lucrative part of a great industry that can and will be further developed and has become a vital part of broadcasting. When television became a reality, the end of AM radio was predicted. Today it is stronger than ever, so the advent of FM radio with a constantly increasing audience will not mean the end of AM radio, but might spur the industry into offering improved programming.

KNEV has been successful because it has offered what a large part of our population wants and will support. Some day the battle for the listening audience may be keener than it is today, but that will depend on the desire of the broadcasters to present programs of more general appeal. There are thousands of listeners who will listen only to rock and roll, and there are thousands of listeners to whom rock and roll has absolutely no appeal—in fact they even resent it. So there are two separate types of audience looking to the radio for entertainment, information, education, news and weather reports. FM has brought a new audience to radio, one that can be developed to a point where it will become an active rival of AM radio.

In Europe, FM is leading, and that is because the majority of sets are equipped to receive FM, which is not true in this country. But throughout the world people are looking for quality, and that makes FM broadcasting definitely an increasingly important factor in the development of an industry that has come a long way in a short time primarily because there is nothing that can replace it. FM is an improvement on AM from the audio standpoint. The elimination of noise and static have had a very definite appeal to listeners, and as more people understand what the difference between AM and FM radio really is, the battle for the listener will become more acute. That is when radio, AM and FM, will show improvement in programming and in transmission, for American genius is never satisfied, always seeking better ways of appealing to the public, always looking for improved ways to attract the dollar.

PART SEVEN

The Sports Bonanza

25. BOB CHEYNE
    Sports Publicity Director, University of Arkansas

26. BERT S. WEST
    Vice President and General Manager, KVI, Seattle, Washington

27. ALLAN NEWMAN
    Program Director, KSFO, San Francisco, California

In recent years, radio stations in the United States, like television stations, have discovered the growing listener appeal of sports programming. Often in many areas, radio stations have been able to broadcast "play-by-play" coverage of an athletic event, and do so exclusively, for the at-home games, as a normal course of events, have been "blacked out" to television.

Not only has play-by-play coverage found growing audience appeal on the nation's radio stations, but other types of sports coverage have occupied increasing segments of broadcast time. Such features as interviews with the players (this is sometimes done in conjunction with listeners' phone-in programs), five-minute commentary by big name athletes, sports news with scores—have all been effective audience builders.

Radio is able to cover all types of sports, ranging from remotes staged in bowling alleys to the annual Soap Box Derby. In smaller towns, the local radio station—and in many cases more than one simultaneously—cover virtually all of the competitive sporting events: football, basketball, and track and field events. Generally, too, radio stations find sporting events highly saleable, for such events generate goodwill for the client's product or service and also offer large diversified audiences.

As television networks and individual TV stations bid staggering sums for coverage rights, radio stations negotiate quietly and often come up with greater access and generally wider coverage.

In this section of the book, three of the nation's real sports specialists tell of the rising appeal of sports on the radio. While all have many things in common with regard to sports and broadcasting, all three have what amount really to three different occupations. One is both a general manager of a very successful major market radio station and also president of a Pacific Coast League baseball team. Another is an illustrious program director, whose station can be ranked easily with the top five sports stations in the United States. The third sits on the other side of the desk—he's an educator and a sports promoter.

All three substantiate the obvious fact that sports, more and more, is a bonanza to modern radio.

25

BOB CHEYNE

Dean of sports publicity directors in the Southwest Conference, Bob Cheyne is in his 18th year at the University of Arkansas. As director of the University of Arkansas Sports Network, he handles the complete operation of the nation's largest university-directed sports radio network.

OF THE THREE major ingredients in radio programming today—news, music and sports—I believe that the world of sports offers perhaps the greatest challenge for improvement of programming and revenue gain in the years ahead. The sports world has entertainment appeal; it rivals regular news in its demand for accuracy and commentary, and it challenges the talents of your staff as well as the finest equipment that radio can provide. As a revenue-producer, it has long been an important factor in our newspaper coverage; and it represents the fastest-growing revenue in the television industry.

As a medium that is instantaneous, mobile, versatile, imaginative and compatible with any format, radio is best suited to provide the best coverage of sports for today's "on-the-go" kind of living.

Broader sports coverage—not just play-by-play—is needed to fill the requirements of an American public that has more time for leisure (figures on participation and on attendance continue to climb). The public is more knowledgeable in the area of sports competition; the field of interest has grown from football, baseball and basketball to golf, bowling, track, the water sports and many others; and there is a significant increase in interest among women in sports today. The public wants sports coverage in depth—as it happens. There is no one special time for sports news on radio.

Developing the Radio "Sports Page"

Radio is a continuous publication—every minute of the day. To present a complete "radio sports page," the total program should approximate newspaper coverage—play-by-play, features, standings and the column. All of this can effectively be done on radio and sponsored as continuing shows. It demands planning, imagination and full use of available remote equipment.

The radio sports page begins with your sports director. If he has the professional ability (not just as a radio announcer but with a background in sports) he can develop a sports image that will make your station in demand.

No matter what your music format and style happens to be, a healthy percentage of your listening audience will enjoy good sports programming. Metropolitan newspapers and national depend upon a solid sports format for revenue and for best audience ratings.

The radio sports director needs to become more involved in his local "sports beat." All too often he is not taken into the confidence of sports personalities within his area because of a lack of contact. Yet, he has much to offer.

Obviously, a 250-watt station can't always afford the budget of a full-time sports director, but I contend that it cannot afford the absence of one man with a solid background in sports. He may have to handle another staff assignment. But the station should allow ample time for him to handle this assignment professionally. This is true in any size market. No matter what the population potential of your market, nearly every station has a strong sports potential.

Programming the Sports Page

Our greatest plus is still our versatility and our ability to be first with the facts. Sports results should be reported by radio as soon as we can possibly get them on the air—particularly if they affect our area. Scoreboard shows, reports of high school athletic events, etc. should be programmed several times during the day at the peak of the seasons.

Where the newspaper column takes 12-16 hours to get today's quote into tmorrow's column, radio can go to the coach's office, the training rooms, the sports publicity office instantly by beep phone or within the hour by tape recording. Sports coverage of local rivals (in state and out of state) can be handled by low cost beep phone on important sports developments.

Local application can be given to controversial stories that have a national or regional impact—if we will take radio to the source (or bring the source to our stations). The NCAA-AAU feud, college football's National Letter of Intent, Little League baseball and many other subjects can be treated effectively by radio if we will visit local coaches, officials and athletes.

Build a reputation for the sports feature as a continuing series on local radio. This has been effective nationally on programs like the Jack Drees "Background-in-Sports." A weekly question-and-answer program with a local coach; how-to-do-it programs on fishing, bowling, golf, etc.; an Athlete-of-the-Month (or week) series can all be incorporated into this type of format.

Don't pass up the opportunity to interview (live or on tape) visiting sports dignitaries that come to your town. It would surprise many of your listeners how many sports figures of national or regional importance come through your area during the year.

Make certain that you cover athletic banquets—especially if the speaker is an important sports personality. You may use only excerpts the next day on tape, but your local newspaper can't duplicate the spoken word in its columns.

Live Coverage of Athletic Events

When it comes to live play by play, radio has long been a champion. The game can be taken anywhere via radio—providing economical coverage of high school and college games.

Major college athletic events vary as to radio network origination—all the way from the "wide open" Big Ten coverage to exclusive one-sponsor networks. Something can be said for each method of operation, but radio should be interested in the most practical, economical production possible.

The University of Arkansas Sports Network is such an operation. Now the largest sports network of its kind in the country (94 stations stretched from one coast to the other in 1966), it provides for locally-sponsored, non-exclusive (in multiple markets within the state) broadcasts at the lowest possible cost to individual stations. There is no "rights fee" as such. The U. of A. hires the personnel to produce the broadcast, orders and pays for all line charges and bills each station on a low-profit basis.

Each station receives personalized schedule placards, a weekly "Razorback Roundup" tape show featuring the head football coach free of charge (it can be sold commercially), complimentary tickets to home games (for in-state and border stations only), promotional tapes and brochures. In this respect the Network is a public relations arm of the U. of A. and is directed by the sports publicity director. Basketball broadcasts and the annual spring football game are handled in similar fashion.

Radio has the right to broadcast on a non-exclusive basis any athletic event that newspapers regularly cover without payment of rights fees. This does not include exclusive coverage. Radio, however, also has the obligation (if it carries such games) to help develop fan interest in these events through broader sports coverage. A better job can be done on selling local school officials on the total sports potential of radio—and on the need for live coverage of local events.

Radio Promotes Attendance at Athletic Events

Surveys have shown that live play-by-play broadcasts of local athletic events—particularly high school events—promote fan interest and thereby stimulate attendance. Be positive in your approach to the value on live play-by-play. Radio invites the new fan, educates and informs the current fan and recovers the former fans more certainly than any other media or planned audience promotion. Not including relatives or the close friends of players, more fans became interested in attending high school games following a radio broadcast than by any other means of communication.

A survey conducted among the civic clubs of my city (with over 350 taking part) revealed the following:

How many attend one or more high school games at home each year? 42%.

How many have ever listened to the broadcast of a local high school game? 67%.

Under good weather conditions, would you rather attend or listen to the broadcast of a home game? Attend: 82%.

Have you ever taken a radio to the game to listen to the broadcast while watching the game? 27%.

Do you feel that the absence of broadcasts of away games could discourage or have any adverse affect upon home attendance? Yes: 65%.

Which factors do you feel play the strongest role in poor attendance at home games?
Losing Season—97%.   Inclement Weather—6%
Lack of Parking—62%.   Radio Broadcasts—4%.
Inadequate Publicity—41%. Ticket Price—1%.
Poor Facilities-Seating—19%.

Here is a positive approach to the problem of a reluctant school board:

Radio broadcasts promote season-book sales (the best fan you can have). These are pre-season sales.

Radio can interest the fan who has never attended—or who has lost interest earlier because of a losing season.

Radio can keep interest alive every week, when a school has that long road trip or two.

Radio personalizes the player and the program as no other medium can.

Radio reaches the shut-in and those physically unable to attend the game because of another commitment.

Radio glamourizes the program with added appeal that encourages participation by your students and student groups.

Radio can serve as an extra public relations aid for other school activities while handling the broadcast of a game.

Radio reaches the fringe areas interesting the fan who does not have a close community identity.

To see what kind of a job you are doing, what the public wants and where you can improve—conduct your own sports survey. It will help you to develop a better sports format; it will convince the reluctant school officials that radio can do a great selling job, and it will sell your advertiser on the value of sports programming.

Tournaments and All-Star Games

A constant source of irritation in some areas because of exorbitant "rights fees," high school tournament and all-star games can be carried in an effective manner. The Arkansas Broadcaster's Association has proved this point. The ABA has a special committee to coordinate both events in the state each year. This committee hires a staff of announcers, etc., orders the lines to each station desiring such a broadcast; and bills each staff on a pro-rata basis at the conclusion of the broadcasts. No "rights fees" are charged, the problem of congestion at the state tournament is avoided and the cost is rock bottom to each station.

In a similar manner, radio stations collectively can do much to improve the quality of facilities available for play-by-play coverage of football and basketball games.

Bob Cheyne

Sports Promotions—a Plus

To complete your radio sports page—and the sports image of your station—add the dimension of sports promotions to news, features and play-by-play. There's nothing new about it—but radio needs to take advantage of this potential. In nearly every case, you can interest a sponsor in these projects.

Co-sponsor tournaments (broadcast some action), including basketball, bowling, amateur golf, etc. You'll be surprised at the interest.

Sponsor worthwhile programs for gun safety, fishing derbies, swimming meets, a "Junior Olympics," athletic trips for kids, end-of-the-season athletic banquets and perhaps an Athlete-of-the-Month award (with a visit by the winner to your station). You're limited only by your imagination and the revenue potential is great.

I don't mean to suggest radical changes in your programming but to call your attention to a legitimate area of interest by your radio public. This versatile medium of radio is limited only by our lack of enthusiasm to look for something new and better.

26

BERT S. WEST

A native of Los Angeles, California, Mr. West is a 1948 graduate of the University of California at Los Angeles where he lettered four years in football and was also captain of the track team. He began his broadcasting career at KNX, Los Angeles and became general manager in 1954. Mr. West joined Golden West Broadcasters at KSFO Radio, San Francisco, in 1955 and became general manager of KVI Radio, Seattle, another Golden West station, in 1960.

THERE ARE a number of people in Seattle who are convinced that I am crazy. They base their opinions on the fact that I recently offered a university the largest sum of money ever bid on a collegiate sports package. My bid for the football and basketball radio broadcast rights of the University of Washington was $71,630. Today, my company's radio station KVI owns those rights. And the question before the house is: Did we pay too much? Maybe so. That was about $11,000 more than the last successful bidder for those rights paid, $20,000 more than the second station offered in the current bidding. Looked at another way, that figure—$71,630—is even more of a shocker. KSFO in San Francisco which, like my station, is a Golden West Broadcasters' property, pays only $25,000 for the football-basketball rights of one of the world's largest universities, the University of California at Berkeley . . . a reasonably athletic school even though the students seem to prefer sit-ins to sit-ups.

Another Golden West station, KMPC in Los Angeles, gets

the football-basketball rights of U.C.L.A., my Alma Mater, and a university that I am happy to say has one of the nation's best football teams and very nearly the best basketball . . . KMPC gets those broadcast rights for less than half of what I will pay the University of Washington.

Now, when you add to this the fact that my station is in this country's 21st market, while KSFO is in the seventh largest market and KMPC in America's second richest market, you have even more reason to ask: Why in the world did he pay $71,630 for the broadcast rights of the Washington Huskies?

Well, I'll tell you why I paid that and will pay the same amount next year . . . and perhaps even more than that the third year. But before I get to my reasons, let's look at the costs of some of the other sports-broadcast rights in this country. In 1966, the 20 American and National League baseball teams took in $17,760,000 from local radio and television outlets. NBC-TV paid about $750,000 for each "Game of the Week." And the Commissioner's office got $3,750,000 from the All-Star game and the World Series. Add it all up and the major league baseball gross was more than $27½ million . . . about $2 million more than they got in 1965.

If the increase in baseball radio-TV rights costs was modest, professional football's and the collegiate price hike can only be described as unblushingly brazen. In 1965, broadcasters paid the gridiron wonder $37,683,875—$8 million more than they paid in 1964 . . . a fat two and a half times the amount charged in 1963. The pigskin is not the only thing that gets inflated in football.

Is over $37½ million dollars a crazy price for football? Yes, crazy, mad, insane . . . but not dumb. Sponsors will pay radio and television about $92 million for those rights. Even so, will I get my $71,630 back and a profit as well? Don't worry about that. Golden West Broadcasters is used to paying sizeable chunks of money for sportscasting privileges. And, we're also used to making a sizeable profit.

In 1966, KSFO paid well over $500,000 for the radio broadcast rights of the San Francisco Giants. KMPC has given the California Angels nearly $750,000 for their rights. On the professional football side, KSFO paid almost $100,000 for the play-by-play of the San Francisco Forty-Niners and KMPC has given the

Los Angeles Rams an even $100,000 for their 1966 rights. In each instance, KMPC and KSFO set up networks of 14 to 18 stations so that the games and the pre and post features can be carried beyond the home area.

Yes, it's true that we pay out a lot of money . . . and it's equally true that we get a lot back. In 1966, the sponsors of the San Francisco Giants games paid KSFO about two and a half times as much money as went for the rights. KMPC got back about two and a quarter times as much as its investment for the Angels broadcasts. The sponsors of the Forty Niner games paid in 232% more than the original investment. The Rams brought a margin of 266%. The college packages are more profitable still. The sponsorships of the UCLA games bring in nearly four times as much as is paid to the university . . . and the same is true of the income from advertisers backing the Golden Bears.

Obviously, not all of this income is pure gravy. There are production and talent fees to be paid. And a considerable bundle of line costs. KSFO and KMPC set up networks of between 14 and 18 stations. The network's stations are paid to carry the play-by-play of the baseball and professional football games. These descriptions of the action are sold to major advertisers by Golden West Broadcasters. The network stations, in turn, pay KSFO and KMPC for the pre- and post-game shows and sell these features to their own advertisers. The network stations also sell the spots adjacent to the pre- and post-game shows on a local basis. Even so, the big end of the profits go to KSFO and KMPC, the stations that purchase the rights and originate the sports broadcasts. There are no networks for the college sportscasts in California, so all of the profits from that source go to the Los Angeles and San Francisco stations. However, KVI will organize a network for the University of Washington, and share a part of its sports income with the cooperating stations.

Ah, but suppose you fail to find a sponsor for a piece of million-dollar sports package? I must admit that there have been times when that dismal prospect has had some of us lying awake nights. But we do sell each piece of these packages and each year we get a little smarter about the way to do it. For one thing, we have long since learned that timebuyers are not the people who buy play-by-play broadcasts . . . or even the pre- and post-games. You have to go to the top. And if you can't get a quick answer from an agency big-wig, you bypass him and go to the client. That's where most of the five and six figures sportscast sales are really made. Many an agency that is cool toward sports broadcasts is serving a client who believes that football, baseball, ice hockey or whatever is the most exciting thing in life. And many clients have gone to one of the local universities . . . hopefully the University of Washington. That little knot in the heartstrings can take care of a lot of problems.

So selling sports on radio is not a real problem. It just shortens your life a few years. Programming sports—that is, fitting it into the schedule—is something else. Imagine having your regular programming interrupted for two to three hours some 180 times a year. That's what major league baseball does. And because of national time differences, the game can crop up most any place—morning, afternoon, early evening or night. The night games are great—what programming could beat an exciting sports broadcast! But games in prime time, that's something else. Especially when you have your prime time solidly sold to spot advertisers. In Los Angeles, for example, baseball games on KMPC pre-empt some 10,000 spot announcements each year. Fortunately, the station is popular with advertisers and they allow KMPC to push about 5,000 of these spots into other time periods.

So much for the difficulties of sports programming. What are the joys? KVI was not in sports to any great degree until 1965. Then we acquired the games of the Seattle Angels, a farm club belonging to the California Angels. Incidentally, our company, Golden West Broadcasters, owns the majority interest in both of these clubs and a partial interest in the Los Angeles Rams. In addition to the Seattle Angels broadcasts, we carried the games of the Seattle Totems, a club in the Western Hockey League. We are carrying both teams again this year.

How have we done in the rating books? Well, not so long ago we were fighting a valiant battle for fourth place in the Seattle-Tacoma market. Today, according to Mediastat, we are the most popular station in our area with men and women between the ages of 18 and 49. A couple of other stations have a slight edge on us with youngsters and oldsters . . . but with the addition of the football and basketball games played by the Washington Huskies, we fully expect to whittle away at that narrow margin.

In San Francisco, a city blessed by an abundance of major sports, KSFO has fared dramatically. When Golden West bought the station it was anything but a Number One property. Like KVI when it was first purchased, its programming was dominated by religion and lethargy. Within two years after Giants baseball had gone on KSFO, the station had doubled its audience. In five years, its audience was three times what it had been in our first year of ownership. Today, all rating services agree that KSFO is very much the Number One station in the Bay Area. Small wonder, then, that Bill Shaw, the manager of KSFO, chooses to call it, with ill-concealed modesty, "The World's Greatest Radio Station." And, in fact, I would agree that it is almost as great as another Golden West station that happens to be located in Seattle.

Obviously, there is more to programming than sportscasts. Sportscasting has helped KVI, KSFO and KMPC tremendously . . . so have strong personalities, good middle-of-the-road music and high-quality newscasting. All are important. But live sports coverage has a special virtue. It brings thousands of listeners to your station who have never tuned you in before. My station is in particular need of that kind of traffic. At 570 on the dial, the bottom end, we can't expect to profit from cross-tuning. That's one of the big reasons why I paid a record sum for the Washington Huskies. There is nothing bigger in sports in the whole Northwest. I want the hundreds of thousands of fans who follow the teams of that great school at my end of the dial. If I never made a penny on those broadcasts, the investment still would have been a very smart one. But I will make a penny, a great many of them, in fact.

Just how big can a radio station's sports audience be? Well, it's too early for me to tell you how well the Huskies will do on KVI, so let's look at the San Francisco story. The 16 stations of the Giants Baseball Network cover an area that is the home of 5,522,100 adults. In the 1965 season, the average rating for a Giants broadcast within that area—an area that stretches from Fresno in mid-California to the Oregon border and halfway across Nevada—was 20.5, a nice rating for a prime-time television show. The average share was 61%. This was the network share. On KSFO itself, these shares run about 80%. In the network area, an average of 1,132,000 adults hear each Giants broadcast. That's more people than live in Houston, Baltimore or Cleveland—including the youngsters who live in those cities. No wonder sponsors willingly pay $400,000 for a third of the play-by-play.

For football the story is strong . . . but not quite as strong as the one I have just told. The 14 station Forty-Niner network averages a 37% share of the audience. The KSFO ratings run around 20% with a 50% share of the listeners. That's a nice thing to have happen to your station each Sunday afternoon for 18 weeks in a row.

As the ratings go, so goes the rate card. In 1956, the KSFO rate card quoted $24 as the one-time rate for a Class A one-minute spot. Now that rate stands at $110—a 317% increase! And, that rate will take another step upward.

There's no doubt about it, sports can make a radio station manager extremely happy. What about sponsors? Do they share this euphoria? Definitely. There is no feature on radio—or on television—that can press home sponsor and product identification so well as a play-by-play sportscast. The companies offering beer, tobacco, soft drinks, gasoline and banking services have shared this conviction for years. But food packagers have been slow to accept sports as a vehicle for their sales messages. Folger's Coffee was the first food product to plunge into the West Coast major sports picture. When they first took up a third of the Giants play-by-play their brand had between a 20% and 25% share of the local coffee market. In less than two years of sponsorship their share of sales was just under 40%.

Even so, Folger's experience didn't convince everyone. When the general manager of the San Francisco office of Armour & Company Meat Products Division suggested that his company use the Giants, the agency, Young and Rubicam, urged that they stick to newspapers. They pointed out that sponsorship of a sports package by a food producer was virtually unknown in the east. To the best of my knowledge A & P, who shared the sponsorship of the New York Giants, has been the only exception. In spite of the agency's negative opinion, Armour bought into the Giants play-by-play. In

1965, the company's Bay Area sales were the highest they had been since World War II . . . and the San Francisco-Oakland distribution area enjoyed the highest increase of any Armour market in the country!

Today, there is an impressive list of food producers and distributors who sponsor Golden West sports features. It includes not only Folger's and Armour, but Del Monte Foods, Farmer John Meats and a leading Southern California food market chain, Alpha Beta.

Why does sports work so well for radio sponsors? It works because it carries the sponsor's messages to listeners with a frequency and authority that makes them stick. A survey conducted for Standard Oil of California showed that 32% of the adults living in the northern California area knew that the Standard Station-Chevron Dealers sponsored the Giants broadcasts; 40% were familiar with the Hamms' Beer commercials; and 47% were very much aware of the spots promoting the use of Folger's Coffee.

These percentages were recorded through a technique using unaided recall. Often people forget to remember . . . so the interviewers jogged their minds by asking this question: "Do you recall hearing an advertisement for a gasoline (or a coffee, or a beer) company during the broadcasts of the Giants games?" With this nudge in the cerebrum, 60% of the adult listeners could recite some of the features of the Standard Oil commercials. Fifty-seven percent remembered the virtues of Hamms Beer. And a whopping 72% knew some of the sales points made in the Folger's Coffee announcements.

So, the advertiser pays his money and gets almost eight months of baseball. Now, what do you do for him, beyond the broadcasts themselves? Well, you post 24-sheet billboards, plaster the backs of buses with posters, run ads in the newspapers, take a page in the baseball club's year books, host his key dealers at a two-day outing in Palm Springs and throw another party at the stadium. In short, you're very much in the promotion and public relations business.

But it's not a one-way street. Not by any means. Consider the impossibility of going to Standard Oil and saying: "I run a radio station and I'd like you to promote it." Oh, sure! But once you have sold Standard or Anheuser Busch or United California Banks a baseball or football package, there's nothing presumptuous about this approach. It isn't brass or gall, it's just unnecessary—for without prompting on your part these advertisers will back your package to the limit.

Standard Oil has some 3,800 service stations in the Angels broadcast area. Some 1,200 of these are in the Los Angeles Metropolitan area. Every one of these stations has a banner on its marquee that promotes the Angels, KMPC and the station's frequency. Money wouldn't buy this because they simply wouldn't sell it to you. In addition, Standard is distributing 500,000 maps showing the best routes to the Anaheim Stadium, the home park of the Angels, and each map calls attention to the broadcasts. And on top of that, Standard has printed and is giving its customers one million schedules carrying all of the broadcast times. In fact, Standard Oil is so enthusiastic about its participation in the Angels broadcasts and its identification with the team itself, that it has spent $1 million building a special scoreboard in the ball park—a scoreboard with a tower that reaches up as high as 23 stories.

Standard's whole-hearted support of the Angels sportscasts is no greater than that of the other sponsors. Each one of them is going all-out to get the maximum value out of this major sports package. Anheuser-Busch has put displays in every market and beverage store that carries its product—and most southern California markets and liquor stores do. The beer company has its own Angels KMPC pocket schedules and is passing them out by the thousands . . . so are the 30 branches of the United California Bank . . . the 50 stores of the Alpha Beta supermarket chain . . . and so are the Dutch Boy Paint stores, the Bonanza Air Lines and the makers of Farmer John Meat Products. Besides, all of these businesses are advertising the Angels broadcasts through window banners, counter cards and any other point of purchase display that will attract attention.

Quite obviously, there are many ways in which it pays to sell a sponsor a major sports package. If he's going to spend that kind of money, and associate himself with something of such great interest to the public, he's going to run as hard as he can to get his money's worth—and while he's running, he'll get an awful lot of mileage out of the dollars that your station invested when you committed yourself to big-time sportscasting.

27

ALLAN NEWMAN

Mr. Newman studied at Ohio State University, attended Mexico City College as an exchange student and graduated from Kent State University in English and Theatre Arts. During college Mr. Newman toured with summer theatres as an actor, and after college became a director. He joined KSFO in 1959, was made production coordinator in 1960 and was appointed program director in January, 1962.

KSFO HAS A great success story with sports coverage. The Giants and Forty-Niners are carried on a 19-station network originating from KSFO with pre- and post-games, all of it fully sponsored. Not being completely altruistic, we make money by carrying sports, not the pure gold that most people think because the cost of contracts does not come cheap, but the real gold in sports is what it has done for the station and what we have done with it.

The important thing is that sports create excitement, audience, and new sponsors. The over-all station must be involved with sports. The station must create color and excitement about the sport, and the sport create excitement and color for the station.

When KSFO first purchased the San Francisco Giants, strangely enough a lot of people in San Francisco thought it wouldn't make it on radio here. In fact, there's a network exec, a former one somewhere, who advised his San Francisco station not to touch them. I think he left radio to head up Edsel production! We needed something to tie them into the station so we took an expression Russ Hodges uses for home runs hit by the Giants. Russ always says, "Bye Bye Baby." We created a corny little song from it that became the anthem of the Giants. It is now played at games, clubs, printed in the paper, records, etc.

About five years ago, the Police Athletic League asked us to play a softball game to raise money for sports equipment for kids. We fielded the KSFO "No Stars." I'm the manager with a consecutive record—five years/five losses. We play the VIPs (the Di Maggios, Joe & Dom, Jake Ehrlich, Herb Caen, the Mayor), and we have celebrities on our team like Alan Sherman and Phyllis Diller. I had Pierre Salinger for third base one year and he let in five runs. I kept telling him he was losing votes each time and now I think I was right. We wanted to tie this in with the station and the sports, so we created a parody on "Bye Bye Baby" and then had an outfit called the "Goodtime Washboard Three" also do some songs for it. Corny again, but it works. The game draws over 10,000 people each year and has become an annual event in San Francisco.

Another way of tying the station in with sports and to promote the personalities is the use we make of ID's within the game. We break away from the net on the hour for 11 seconds and we make use of this time to plug all we can. A lot of baseball and football listeners never listen to anything else but sports. We look for all ways possible to brainwash this type of listener to stay with the station. One way that has been successful for us is using the sportscasters themselves to promote the personalities within the game, again making use of the 11-second ID. These are very simple but some fans hearing Russ Hodges or Lon Simmons talking about Don Sherwood or one of our other guys might say to themselves! "If Russ likes him, then it's OK by me."

As I said before, we have a 15-minute Sports Show seven days a week at 5:45 P.M. Six days a week the "Sports Roundup" with Lon Simmons and Sunday "Sports Comprehensive" with Russ Hodges. The Sunday show is a wrap-up of everything that's happened in the past week.

We have a phone show with the vice president of the Giants, Chub Feeney, and anybody that has questions or gripes can talk to the vice president himself. The response has been so excellent on this that on the second show the phone calls jammed the complete exchange, and there was a short period there when there were no phone calls coming into the station. As you may have found, there's no one who can ask more questions than a sports fan. We plan to follow this up during football season with the manager or coach of the Forty-Niners.

We handle our college sports the same way, tying in with the station and promoting them in every way possible. In the past couple of years, we've arranged for our personalities to do the color on some of these games—in fact sometimes I even get into the action of the game.

So the gist of the story is that sports can be a bonanza. It brings in new sponsors and puts you in the position to get them to stay on. It builds new audience, but you have to hold them by tying in the station with sports and tying the over-all package into the community. In smaller communities local sports can even do this better for you, and it can be promoted the same way. Sometimes I take all the deejays to a game, and their talk on the air before and after is great for the station. One of our personalities does special shows on music picked by the players. Little things, but they work!

All of this isn't an entity in itself. It is a part of the station. We have never allowed ourselves to be called a "sports station." We're music, news, personalities and sports. One does not overpower the other. But we have a ball with our sports. It creates excitement for the over-all station that's meant not only profits but the important thing for making profits—audience!

There are even more promotions to be done with community sports because you gamble with less money and in many ways you have more freedom to play around with it. Major league teams can be a bit touchy about various promotions and how they're handled. I've heard radio stations make the Soap Box Derby sound like the Grand Prix, and there's a small station in California that makes a frog jump sound like Ben Hur. It's done the same way—be it Giants or Little League. If your station has a sound of excitement, color and humor, and the sport becomes a part of it, you've got the answer. Come to think of it, I watched the "First Annual Terra Linda Worm Race" in my neighborhood last year and it was kind of exciting!

INDEX

ABC Network, 53, 144
Ace, Goodman, 141
Advertisers: and country music, 109, 122; on sports programs, 167–70; on WPIX-FM Radio, 142
Advertising, 108–09, 134; newspaper, 79, 80
Advertising Age, Summer Workshop of, 109
Allen, Fred, 127
Allen, Garrett, 140
AM radio stations, number of, 74
AM Report, on WEEI Radio, 24
Anderson, Bill, 107
Announcement, 66; political, 114
Announcer, 114
Apollo Project, radio reports on, 24
ARB audience studies, 142, 143

Arkansas Broadcasters' Association, 160
Arnold, Eddy, 107, 117, 121
Ash, Merrill M., 15 *ff.*
Associated Press, 16, 65, 66
Atkins, Chet, 117
"Audio sig cut," for WRYT Radio, 130
Automobile Club, 43

"Background-in-Sports" program, 157
Banjo, in country music, 103
Barrett, John R., 83 *ff.*
Bartley, Robert, quoted, 145
Bascom, Perry B., 89 *ff.*

Bat Kits, 86
Batman, 86, 87
Battle of New Orleans, The, 102
Beatles, 95, 106
"Beautiful" music, 127–30, 132, 134; defined, 127–28
Beck, Dave, 16
Beeper phone, 21–22, 64, 75
Bell Telephone Hour, 121
Bellmont Curve, WVMC Radio editorial on, 68
Benzaquin, Paul, 24, 25
Berkshire Eagle, 50, 51, 52, 55
Bernstein, Leonard, 95
"Big Story," on WVMC Radio, 71
Billboard, 105, 107, 110
Bluegrass music, 103; defined, 110
Blues, 91, 106
"Bob Kennedy/Contact" show, on WBZ Radio, 92
Bond, Gil, 133 *ff.*
Borman, Jim, 42 *ff.*
"Broadcast Pioneers," 34
Broadcasting, Special Report by, 104
Bruton, Robert, 146 *ff.*
Business newscast, 24, 65
Business Week, 118

"C & W Sweeps Grammys" (*Chicago Sun Times*), 105
Cacavas, John, 110
California State Associated Press Award for Merit, 88
Capp, Al, 26
"Careers Unlimited," on KPOJ Radio, 36
Cashbox, 105
Castle Jazz Band, 36
CBS Network, 29, 30, 43, 44

CBS-FM Program Service, 144
CFGM Radio, Toronto, 121
Charlotte Music Club, 35
Cheyne, Bob, 155 *ff.*
Chicago Sun Times, 105
Chicago Sunday American, 105
Chicago Tribune, 72
Christian, Lynn A., 139 *ff.*
Christmas Day programming, 40
Ciardi, John, 35
"Civic Theatre on the Air," on KPOJ Radio, 36
Cline, Patsy, 103
Cluster system, 128–29
Cobb, Everett B., 149 *ff.*
Collins tape deck, 147
Commercials, 77, 79, 114, 129, 132; exotic, 129; limited, 84
Community Pride Award, sponsored by WBT Radio, 34
Congressional Record, 33
"Country A-Go-Go" show, on WENO Radio, 121
"Country AM's Go To Town" (*Variety*), 105
Country music, 91, 94, 96, 101–11, 113, 115, 116–23; and advertisers, typical, 109, 122; continental, 111; defined, 105; demographic studies of listeners to, 122; evolution of, 105–06; future of, 109–10; instrumentation for, 102–03, 107, 110, 111, 117; modern, 110; and number of records sold, 103; patriotic, 117; pure, 110; range of, 106
Country Music Association, 104, 107, 109, 122
"Country Music Goes To Town" (Sunday *Chicago Sun Times*), 105

Index

Crime Investigating Committee, Senate, 16
Crump, George, 120

De Vaney, Ken, 84
Dean, Jimmy, 107
Dickens, Little Jimmy, 121
Director: news, 20, 21, 77, 79; program, 131–32, 133; sports, 156
Disc jockey, 17, 26, 86, 102, 118
Distinguished Service Award, of NAB, 37
Dixieland, 90
Dobro guitar, in country music, 102
Documentary, 88, 92
Don't Let the Stars Get in Your Eyes, 102
Draft, KRLA Radio's study of, 88
Drees, Jack, 157
Drums, in country music, 102, 107, 110
Dubinetz, George G., 104 *ff.*
Dudley, Dave, 117

Easter Egg Hunt, WENO Radio's, 121
Editor, news, 29, 66
Editorial, radio, 32–33, 39–40, 54, 61, 68, 92
Electric guitar, in country music, 107
Electronics Industries Association, 142
Ellis, Elmo, 140
Emerson, Ralph Waldo, quoted, 61
Everly Brothers, 106

Fairness doctrine, 32, 72
Federal Communications Commission, 77, 80, 84, 141
Fiddle, in country music, 102, 110
Five string banjo, in country music, 103
Flatt & Scruggs, 103
FM radio, 139–52; advancing property values of, 145; number of sets, 142–43; number of stations, 74, 144; and satellite transmission, 144; stereo, 139, 140, 143, 144; syndication services for, 144
Folk music, 103, 106, 110; *see also* Country music
Fondren, Lee, 144
Free Europe, Radio, 33
Freedom Foundation, 33
French horn, in country music, 107
Fulbright, J. W., 35

Gambling, John, Jr., 141
General Electric Company, 24
George Washington Honor Medal, 33
Georgia Pacific Corporation, 62–63
Gillett, Rupert, 32
Girls' records, 114
Glaser, Jerry, 120 *ff.*
Golden, Harry, 33
Golden West Broadcasters, 162, 163, 164, 165, 166, 168
Gray, Barry, 141
Green Berets, on WBT Radio, 34
Greene, Bill, 144
Griffin, Merv, 121
"Growing Sound of Country Music" (*Broadcasting's* Special Report), 104

Guitar, in country music, 102, 106, 107, 110

Haas, Julian, 62 *ff.*
Harp, in country music, 107
Hayman, Richard, 110
Helicopter reports, 120
Hillbilly music, 101, 103, 120; *see also* Country music
Hodges, Russ, 172
Hoedown music, 103; *see also* Country music
"Hometown News," on KAGH Radio, 65
Hooper ratings, 97, 143, 148
Horse shows, 113
Howard, Jan, 107
Hullabaloo, 121
Human interest stories, 78–79
Humor, 86, 87, 129
Humphrey, Hubert H., 44
Hurlbut, John H., 67 *ff.*
Husky, Ferlin, 121

IGM, as pioneer in syndication, 144
Interpretive reporting, 24
Interview, 17, 65, 78, 79
Iowa Radio Network, 76, 78

Jackson, Richard, 49 *ff.*
Jacob's Pillow Dance Festival, 51
James, Sonny, 107
Jardine, William, 75
Jazz, 36, 90, 91

"Jefferson High School Convocation" series, on WBT Radio, 35
Johnson, Lyndon B., 44
Jones, George, 117
Juvenile delinquency, radio news coverage of, 58

KAGH Radio, Crossett, Arkansas, 62–66
Kalb, Marvin, 35
KATR Radio, Eugene, Oregon, 112–15
KBRG-FM Radio, San Francisco, 144
Kennedy, Robert F., 16
KGBS Radio, Los Angeles, 118, 123
KHJ Radio, Los Angeles, 84
KIBW-FM Radio, Wichita, 140
Kilburn, Lorelei, 71
KIXI Radio, Seattle, 131–32, 134, 135
KIXL-FM, Dallas, 140
KLTF Radio, Little Falls, Minnesota, 56
KLZ-FM Radio, Denver, 144
KMOX Radio, St. Louis, 34
KMPC Radio, Los Angeles, 162–63, 164, 165, 166, 169
KNEV-FM Radio, Reno, 149–51
KNUZ Radio, Houston, 140
KODA-FM Radio, Houston, 140
KPOJ Radio, Portland, Oregon, 36–41
KQE-FM Radio, Houston, 140
KRAK Radio, Sacramento, 123
Krelstein, Harold, 107
KRLA Radio, Pasadena, California, 84–88

Index

KSFO Radio, San Francisco, 162, 163, 164, 166, 167, 171, 172
KSON Radio, San Diego, 101
KVI Radio, Seattle, 162, 164, 165, 166
KWPC Radio, Muscatine, Iowa, 75–78

Lawrence, Mike, 79
Lazarsfeld, Paul, 84
Lear Jet Stereo Cartridge, 143
Lemme, John H., 56 ff.
Libel, 66
Life magazine, 103, 104
LSD, KRLA Radio's study of, 88

McClendon, Gordon, 144
McKinnon, Dan, 101 ff., 120
Maltby, Richard, 110
Manager: news, 29; sales, 77, 133; station, 76, 77, 79
Marijuana, KRLA Radio's study of, 88
Marion, Paul B., 27 ff.
Martin, Dean, 118
Mayor's Award for Community Service, 34
Mead, Margaret, 35
Mediastat audience studies, 143, 165
Melton, Erv, 29
Metromedia FM stations, 144
Miller, Roger, 117, 118, 121
Minneapolis Star & Tribune, 75
Modern music, 83–86, 89–91, 92, 93–97; defined, 94–95
Mondale, Walter F., 43
Monroe, Bill, 103

"Mood into," on WRYT Radio, 130
Morris, Dave, 139, 140
Mt. Carmel Daily Republican Register, The, 71–72
Mueller, Vern, 36 ff.
Murrow, Edward R., quoted, 37
Music: "beautiful," *see* Beautiful music; bluegrass, *see* Bluegrass music; country, *see* Country music; defined, 93–94; folk, 103, 106, 110 (*see also* Country music); hillbilly, 101, 103, 120 (*see also* Country music); hoedown, 103 (*see also* Country music); Mexican, 117; modern, *see* Modern music; pop, 83, 89, 94, 96 (*see also* Modern music); religious, 96, 114; western, *see* Western music
Musicpac, 144

NAB (National Association of Broadcasters), 37, 87, 145
Narcotics, KRLA Radio's study of, 88
"Nashville, Home of Country and Western" (*Chicago Sunday American*), 105
Nashville sound, 117, 118, 119
National Association of Broadcasters (NAB), 37, 87, 145
National Association of FM Broadcasters, 143
NBC Network, 144
Nelskog, Wally, 131 f.
New York ARB Radio Study (1966), 142
Newcomb, Alan, 32, 33
Newman, Allan, 171 ff.
News, 15–22, 24, 27–28, 37–39, 41,

42–45, 51–55, 63–66, 87, 92, 114; announcement used in, 66; balance in, 28; business, 24, 65; on CBS Network, 29; equipment for gathering, 21–22, 30, 31, 75; food, 24; of foreign countries, 78; health, 24; immediacy of, 57–58, 60, 65; manpower for coverage of, 21; political, 28, 31; of public disasters, 37; science, 24; and "showmanship" as interference with, 21; small market, 56 ff., 61, 66, 67; speed of handling, 79; sports, *see* Sports news; on TV, 29, 30; young people interested in, 87
News director, 20, 21, 77, 79
News editor, 29, 66
News flow, 44
News manager, 29
News reporter, 19–21, 38
Newspapers, and radio broadcasting, 71–73, 75
Newsweek, 104, 105
North Adams Transcript, 50
North American Service, of Radio Moscow, 31
Nutrition, Harvard's Department of, 24
Nyaradi, Nicholas, 33

O'Connor, Norman, 26
Ode to the Little Brown Shack Out Back, 103
"Open Line News," on WEBC Radio, 53
Organ, electric, in country music, 107
Owens, Buck, 95, 117

Page, Patti, 103
Parkinson, F. Geer, 127 ff.
Peabody Award, 36
Peterson, Dale, 116 ff.
Peyton Place, 121
Piano, in country music, 102, 110 117
Pittsburgh Press, The, 129
PIX-Mix formula, 141
Plough Broadcasting, Inc., 107, 122, 123
PM Report, on WEEI Radio, 24
Political news, 28, 31
Pop music, 83, 89, 94, 96; *see also* Modern music
Program director, 131–32, 133
Programming, radio, *see* Radio programming
"Project 60" series, on WBT Radio, 33
Prologue (stereo music service), 144
Propaganda, and Radio Moscow, 31
Public-affairs programming, 31–35, 36, 53, 55, 58, 60
Pulse ratings, 25, 97, 108, 115, 122, 123

Quality Media, Inc., 143
Quinn, Dominic R., 23 ff.

Radio Free Europe, 33
Radio journalism, top national award for, 32
"Radio Moscow," on WBT Radio, 31, 32

Radio programming: musical, *see* Music; of news, *see* News; of public affairs, 31–35, 36, 53, 55, 58, 60; of "radio sports page," 157 (*see also* Sports news)
Radio receivers, number of, 74–75
Radio-TV Mirror Gold Medal, 33
Ragtime, 90
Rather, Dan, 44
Receivers, radio, number of, 74–75
Record Industry Association of America, 107
Record requests, for top 40 program, 85–86
Reeves, Jim, 102, 117
Remington, Fred, 129
Remotes, 55, 76, 114
Reporter, 19–21, 38
Reporting, interpretive, 24
"Rights fees," and ABA, 160
Robbins, Marty, 117
Rock and roll, 17, 90, 91, 94, 96, 129, 139, 151
Rockability, defined, 110
Roosevelt, Franklin D., 70

Sales Executives and Marketing Club, 109
Sales manager, 77, 133
Satellite transmission, of FM stereo, 144
Satisfied Mind, 102
Saturday Evening Post, 104
Saxophone, in country music, 117
Schofield, Dick, 122
Science news, 24
Seaborg, Glenn, 35
Senate Crime Investigating Committee, 16

Shafer automated system, 147
Shepherd, Ed, 77–78
Sigma Delta Chi, 32
Simmons, Lon, 172
Sindlinger & Company, 75
Singleton, Shellby, 116
Sixteen Tons, 102
Smallens, Alex, 144
"Sound Off," on WBEC Radio, 54
"Spanish News," on Iowa Radio Network, 78
Spectrum, three-part, of KIXI Radio, 134
Sponsor Magazine, 116
"Sports Comprehensive," on KSFO Radio, 172
Sports director, 156
Sports news, 55, 155–73; attendance at athletic events promoted by, 159–60; as bonanza, 173; live coverage of, 158, 166, 167; and payment for broadcast rights, 162–64; and "radio sports page," 156–57, 161; sponsors of, 167–70; and sports promotions, 161
"Sports Roundup," on KSFO Radio, 172
Stafford, Jo, 103
Standard Rate and Data Service, 134
Starr, Kay, 103
Station manager, 76, 77, 79
Steel guitar, in country music, 102, 110
Steinberg, William, 129
Storer Broadcasting, Inc., 123
Stratton, Ron, 54
Stringers, 28, 29, 30, 78
Strings, sweeping, in country music, 107, 110
Surfing reports, 120
Swing, 90

Talk programs, 24, 25-26, 77
Tanglewood Music Festival, 51
Tape recorder, 17, 22, 57, 58, 59, 64
"Target" series, on WBT Radio, 33
"Teenage Underground," on WRYT Radio, 129
Telephone, in radio news coverage, 57, 59, 65
Telephone program, 25, 26, 40, 77
"Thomas Jefferson High School Convocation" series, on WBT Radio, 35
Thomlinson, R. E. "Bob," 112 ff.
Time magazine, 104
Top 40 program, 83, 84, 85, 96; see also Modern music
Transistor mixer, at WBT Radio, 31
Triangle Audio Program Service, 144
Trombone, in country music, 107

UFO sightings, KRLA Radio's study of, 88
University of Arkansas Sports Network, 158
UPI "Best Editorial" Award, 33
USIA, 33

Van Doren, Mark, 35
Variety, 104
Vetter, Charles, 33
Vietnam veterans, on WBT Radio, 34
Violin, in country music, 117
Volger, George J., 74 ff.
Volpe, John A., 54

Wabash Valley College Foundation, 69
WABC Radio, New York, 141
WABC-FM Radio, New York, 140
Watts riot, KRLA Radio's analysis of, 88
WBAP Radio, Fort Worth, 146
WBT Radio, Charlotte, 27-35
WBZ Radio, Boston, 89-93
WCBS Radio, New York, 141
WCCO Radio, Minneapolis, 42-45
Weather Bureau, United States, 38
WEBC Radio, Pittsfield, Massachusetts, 50-55
WEEI Radio, Boston, 23-26
Welk, Lawrence, 26
Wells, Kitty, 103
WENO Radio, Nashville, 121
West, Bert S., 162 ff.
Western music, 91, 94, 96, 105, 107, 109, 110, 113, 116, 118, 120; defined, 110; see also Country music
WFAA Radio, Dallas, 146, 147
WFAA-FM Radio, Dallas, 147, 148
WFMX Radio, Statesville, North Carolina, 140
Wheeler, Billy Ed, 103
Whitaker, Charles, 141
Whiteman, Paul, 95
Williams, Danny, 93 ff.
Wilson, Steve, 71
Windsor, Walter, 144
WINS Radio, New York, 141
WJJD Radio, Chicago, 107-09, 122
WJRZ Radio, Newark, 123
WKY Radio, Oklahoma City, 93
WLS-FM Radio, Chicago, 144
WMAL-FM Radio, Washington, 140
WMCA Radio, New York, 141
WNBC Radio, New York, 141

Index

WNEW Radio, New York, 141
WNEW-FM Radio, New York, 144
"Woman of the Year" Award, sponsored by WBT Radio, 34
WOR Radio, New York, 141
WPAT Radio, New York, 141
WPIX-FM Radio, New York, 141–42
WPLO Radio, Atlanta, 123
WQXR Radio, New York, 141
WRFM Radio, New York, 145
WRYT Radio, Pittsburgh, 127–30
WSB-FM Radio, Atlanta, 140
WSDM-FM Radio, Chicago, 144
WTHE Radio, Long Island, New York, 123
WVMC Radio, Mt. Carmel, Illinois, 68–73
WWVA Radio, Wheeling, 123

Young people, news material interesting to, 87
Your Cheatin' Heart, 102